PRINCE FREDERICK OF HOMBURG

Heinrich von Kleist

TRANSLATED FROM THE GERMAN

BY

L. ROBERT SCHEUER

WITH AN INTRODUCTION

BY

ANNA M. ROSENBERG

Department of Modern Languages
Memorial University of Newfoundland
St. John's, Newfoundland, Canada

BARRON'S EDUCATIONAL SERIES, INC.
GREAT NECK, NEW YORK

Library of Congress Catalog Card No. 61-18365

INTRODUCTION

In 1801, when the twenty-four-year-old Heinrich von Kleist, having resigned his Prussian army commission two years before, started pouring his tensions, his torments, his violence, and his tenderness into poetic works, German literature stood at what is now usually considered the end of the Classic and the beginning of the Romantic period. Such fundamentally Classic works as Schiller's *Braut von Messina* and *Wilhelm Tell* and the first part of Goethe's *Faust* were published between 1801, when Kleist started writing, and 1811, when he died. The same years saw the publication of works which are usually called Romantic, such as Friedrich von Schlegel's poems, Fouqué's *Undine,* and the Arnim and Brentano collection of folk poetry, *Des Knaben Wunderhorn.* Kleist, even more than other poets, defies any effort to classify him; in fact his works contain such realism and such psychological subtlety that he seems to belong to the twentieth century as well as to the nineteenth. It is therefore not surprising that this poet, of whom so many contemporaries violently disapproved, is now accepted as one of the great masters of German literature.

As a young ensign in the Prussian army, Kleist had taken part in the First Coalition war against France, and later the Napoleonic wars overshadowed his life. He witnessed the Prussian collapse at Jena, spent six months as a French prisoner under suspicion of espionage, and accompanied

Austria's rebellion against Napoleon with stirring patriotic lyrics. He saw Napoleon's defeat at Aspern and later had his hopes shattered by Austria's defeat at Wagram. It was the sincere desire of his last years to help rouse Prussia against the invader. Just before starting work on *Prinz Friedrich von Homburg* he declared his intention to write a number of plays which would strike into the heart of his time. But *Prinz Friedrich von Homburg* was neither published nor performed until ten years after Kleist's death, and Kleist did not live to see Napoleon's defeat and Prussia's regeneration.

Kleist was born in 1777 in Frankfurt-an-der-Oder into an aristocratic Prussian family. The son of an army officer, he was destined for a military career; he entered a Potsdam regiment at fifteen, went to war, and was made a lieutenant at twenty. Already it was abundantly clear that he was in the wrong element, and his growing distaste for military life caused him to ask for his release in 1799 "in order to complete his studies," which he proceeded to do with the eagerness, thoroughness, and single-mindedness which characterized all his activities. The same year he became engaged to a childhood friend, Wilhelmine von Zenge.

Kleist was anxious to make up for his wasted years as a soldier, to form himself into the kind of person he was meant to be; and his studies were explicitly designed to help him master his life, to guide him in the design of a life plan, without which life seemed to him undignified and contemptible. During his studies of philosophy he came into contact with the works of Kant, which made a great and shattering impression on him and destroyed his naive belief that if only he studied enough he would surely find supreme eternal truth. If perfect truth was unattainable to the human intellect, then the future lay black before him, and he had no aim. The impact of Kant's ideas as he understood them completely upset Kleist's whole philosophy of life and brought him close to despair — but out of this crisis the poet was born.

Here starts the pattern which is repeated over and over again in Kleist's life: when he is torn within himself he changes his abode, he starts travelling as if to find peace of mind in some other place. His flight took him to countless places in Germany, France, and Switzerland. In 1802 he decided to buy a Swiss farm and to live a natural life in Rousseau's sense, a decision which led to the dissolution of his engagement as his fiancée felt herself "too weak for the duties of a farmer's wife." The farm was never bought, and his travels continued.

All this time he wrote furiously, with abandon and without sparing himself. His first work, *Die Familie Schroffenstein,* was finished. He now realized his poetic powers and with boundless ambition demanded too much of himself — he felt capable of writing a tragedy such as the world had long been waiting for, a tragedy which would combine the best of the Greek and the Shakespearean drama. How close he came to fulfilling this ambition in his grand tragedy *Robert Guiskard* is a matter of wistful speculation: despairing of his ability to succeed, he burned the manuscript, together with many other writings, and disappeared. He was later found in Boulogne trying to join Napoleon's armies which were about to invade England, an avowedly suicidal intention and particularly hard to explain in view of his strong dislike of Napoleon.

His health broke down shortly after, and he did not recover until many months later, when he returned to his family. To please them, he tried to refrain from writing poetry and accepted a Civil Service position, which took him to Königsberg in 1805; but the year after he left this post again to live on his earnings as an author. He now wrote the comedy, *Der Zerbrochene Krug,* and *Amphitryon,* an adaptation of Molière's comedy, which in Kleist's hands became a mystic erotic drama; also several short stories of great power, in which he used a strong, closely knit prose entirely his own. His greatest story, *Michael Kohlhaas,* was started at that time.

A journey into occupied Berlin a few months after Prussia's defeat at Jena led to his imprisonment by the French authorities, during which he worked on the daring and brilliant tragedy, *Penthesilea.* After his release he went to Dresden, where for a short period he found both friendship and appreciation of his work. "I wish you were here," he wrote to his sister Ulrike, "to be happy with me and to see all this yourself." Together with a friend, Adam Müller, he started a literary periodical, "Phöbus," in which many of his own writings appeared, including a rewritten fragment of *Robert Guiskard.* Humbly he submitted the first issue to Goethe, inviting his opinion and expressing the hope that he might contribute to the magazine. Goethe's cool refusal did much to seal "Phöbus' " fate, and indeed the twelfth volume, which appeared early in 1809, was the final one.

Goethe's attitude is not really surprising. Conscious of the value of self-limitation, full of affirmation of life, steeped in classical tradition, serene and calm, he was frightened and shocked by the boundlessness of Kleist's works, his preoccupation with death, his impatient disregard of limits, the violence of his emotions, and the intemperate tone of such works as *Penthesilea*. Goethe may have known that Kleist had once vowed in youthful impetuosity "to wrest the laurels from Goethe's brow;" but even if he did not, the clashing contrast of the two personalities would be sufficient to explain his attitude. Some critics feel that in his works Kleist recklessly released dangerous tensions which Goethe had painfully learned to keep under control, and that Kleist's violence frightened Goethe because he felt with great sensitivity just what Kleist meant and feared for his own equilibrium. Be that as it may, we know that Goethe recognized Kleist's genius ("This is no ordinary talent," he said) and tried to be fair; he even produced Kleist's comedy, *Der Zerbrochene Krug,* but the single performance was a signal failure, led to some uncomfortable moments for Goethe, and did nothing to relieve the tension between the two poets. Goethe's disapproval contributed much to the lack of appreciation which Kleist encountered during his lifetime, for Goethe's word commanded profound respect in the literary world.

But Kleist continued to write. *Das Käthchen von Heilbronn* and *Die Hermannsschlacht* were finished in 1808, and in 1810 he completed his last play, *Prinz Friedrich von Homburg.* In this work Kleist combined, and controlled, his abundant talents: his sense of drama, gift for poetry, deep psychological insight, and command of language and meter. But in spite of this demonstration of artistic maturity he encountered nothing but frustration in the outside world.

After an unsuccessful attempt to produce a weekly paper in Prague, he started in 1810 to publish Berlin's first daily newspaper, "Die Berliner Abendblätter." When that enterprise also failed, largely owing to difficulties with government censorship, Kleist at thirty-four found himself penniless, without a job or the prospect of one, his work unappreciated by his contemporaries, his country defeated and occupied, and himself completely rejected by his family as a useless member of society, unworthy of sympathy. Even his favorite sister, Ulrike, who had been closest to him and had spent her patrimony in helping him throughout his life, finally seemed to turn against him. *Prinz Friedrich von Homburg* had been presented to the Prussian Court, but Court circles disapproved of the "ignoble" part Homburg played and prevented the production.

The offer of a double suicide from Henriette Vogel, the incurably sick wife of a Prussian official, came as a welcome promise of release from a life which had become unbearable, and with feelings of "indescribably happy serenity" Kleist shot first her and then himself, in the fall of 1811, at the shores of Lake Wannsee, near Potsdam.

Prinz Friedrich von Homburg was not published until 1821. In the same year it was produced in Vienna, but the police closed the play after five performances: Archduke Charles felt it would demoralize his army. Homburg's breakdown in the face of death upset the hallowed conventions of heroism.

Yet, the very scene in which the Prince renounces glory,

career, and love and loses self-control and self-respect is the high dramatic point of the play. Up to this crisis Homburg's personality was not real but full of conventional illusions; he was a fairy-tale hero, a story-book hero, and lived in a dream world. With profound poetic artistry Kleist shows him first in a trance-like sleep in a lovely romantic moonlight setting. At the sight of his open grave, in one moment of supreme and humiliating reality, the sham falls away. At this point the wise Elector shows him that he is the master of his own fate, and the hero awakens and attains stature. He matures before our eyes, and we see the emergence of a truly heroic personality, living in reality and worthy to be a leader. And where before the thought of death was unbearable because he had not yet really lived and had nothing to die for, he now can renounce life freely and serenely, in full understanding of the issues at stake. And now the Elector may pardon him — for to execute him would be folly and waste.

This pardon is significant, for the play shows not only the subordination of an individual to a greater law but also a great and wise ruler who recognizes that the community stands and falls by the freedom which it allows to the individual, and indeed by the stature of the individual for whom and by whom it exists. This mature outlook on the rights and duties of the individual and of the state is at variance with the Prussian spirit as the world has come to think of it. We have here a patriotic play, but one in which the relationship of individual freedom to the law and the interweaving of illusion and reality are treated with deep understanding and amazing economy of words. It is at the same time so poetic that we can agree with Heinrich

Heine, who said that the play seemed to him "as if written by the very spirit of poetry."

The accompanying translation attempts to convey this spirit by following the phrase and meter of the original. But even a prose translation used by a French theatrical company in the 1950's proved to be a great success. Interest in the play continues to spread. Kleist has joined the ranks of those whose genius, long after their lonely and misunderstood life is over, is finally appreciated by later generations.

MEMORIAL UNIVERSITY OF NEWFOUNDLAND,

Anna M. Rosenberg

April 1961.

TRANSLATOR'S ACKNOWLEDGMENTS

The translator owes thanks to his wife, Lucille Scheuer, and to Professor Franz Werneke of Göttingen University for their encouragement and criticism.

CHARACTERS

FREDERICK WILLIAM: *Elector of Brandenburg*
THE ELECTRESS: *Frederick William's wife*
PRINCESS NATALIA OF ORANGE: *the Elector's niece, chief of a regiment of dragoons*

MARSHAL DÖRFLING
PRINCE FREDERICK ARTHUR OF HOMBURG: *general of the cavalry*
COLONEL KOTTWITZ: *of the regiment of the Princess of Orange*

HENNINGS:
COUNT TRUCHSS: } *colonels of the infantry*
COUNT HOHENZOLLERN: *of the Elector's suite*

CAPTAIN GOLZ:
COUNT GEORGE OF SPARREN:
STRANZ: } *captains of the cavalry*
SIEGFRIED OF MÖRNER:
COUNT REUSS:

A SERGEANT MAJOR

OFFICERS, CORPORALS AND HORSEMEN, COURTIERS, LADIES-IN-WAITING, PAGES, HAIDUKS, SERVANTS, PEOPLE OF ALL AGES

ACT ONE

SCENE ONE

Fehrbellin. Garden in the old French style. In the background a castle, with a ramp leading down into the garden. It is night.

The PRINCE OF HOMBURG, *bareheaded, with open shirt, half awake and half asleep, sits under an oak tree, winding a wreath. The* ELECTOR, *the* ELECTOR'S WIFE, PRINCESS NATALIA, COUNT HOHENZOLLERN, CAPTAIN GOLZ, *and* OTHERS *secretly step out of the castle and look down on the* PRINCE *from the railing of the ramp.* PAGES *with torches.*

COUNT HOHENZOLLERN
    The Prince of Homburg, our courageous cousin,
    who with his horsemen in the past three days
    has led the fleeing Swedes a merry chase
    and just today again, still out of breath,
    reported to the staff at Fehrbellin —
    your orders to him were that he remain
    a mere three hours for provender and then
    at once move forward to the Hackel Mountains,
    again opposing Wrangel, who has tried
    to fortify himself along the Rhyn?

1

THE ELECTOR

That's so.

HOHENZOLLERN

      All chiefs of squadrons duly ordered
to move from town, as planned, at ten tonight,
he falls exhausted, panting like a hound,
upon the straw to rest his limbs a little
before the battle facing us at dawn.

THE ELECTOR

I know that. Well?

HOHENZOLLERN

          As now the hour arrives
and all the cavalry is mounted and the horses
trample the field before the gates,
who's missing? — Its commander, Prince of Homburg.
They look for him with torches, lights, and lanterns
and find him —
(*He takes a torch from a* PAGE.)
          look yourself: somnambulating,
as never you'd believe, upon that bench,
attracted by the moonlight in his sleep.
Envisioning posterity, he's busy
entwining his own splendid wreath of glory.

THE ELECTOR

What?

HOHENZOLLERN

      Yes, indeed. Look down here: there he sits.
(*He lets the light of the torch fall on the* PRINCE.)

THE ELECTOR

Immersed in sleep? Absurd!

HOHENZOLLERN

                              Yes, fast asleep.
You call him by his name and he falls down.
(*pause*)

THE ELECTRESS

The young man must be ill, upon my life!

PRINCESS NATALIA

He needs a doctor.

THE ELECTRESS

                    I think we should assist him,
not spend the moment making fun of him.

HOHENZOLLERN (*handing back the torch*)

Oh, he is well, my sympathetic ladies;
as well as I, by God! The Swede tomorrow
will feel it when we meet him in the field.
It's nothing more, believe me on my word,
than just a wayward habit of his mind.

THE ELECTOR

A fairy-tale I thought it. — Follow, friends,
and let us take a closer look at him.
(*They descend from the ramp.*)

A COURTIER (*to the* PAGES)

Keep back the torches!

HOHENZOLLERN

                         Let them, let them, friends!
If all the town were going up in flames,
his senses would perceive of it no more
than would the stone he's wearing on his finger.
(*They surround the* PRINCE; *the* PAGES *provide light.*)

THE ELECTOR (*bending over him*)

What are the leaves he's twining? Willow leaves?

HOHENZOLLERN

What? Willow leaves, Sire? Laurel leaves they are,
as he has seen them on the heroes' paintings
that hang within the armory in Berlin.

THE ELECTOR

Where did he find the laurel in our sand?

HOHENZOLLERN

God knows.

THE COURTIER

Perhaps back in the garden; there
the gardener raises other foreign plants.

THE ELECTOR

It's strange, by heaven! Still, I think I know
what agitates the breast of this young fool.

HOHENZOLLERN

Of course the battle of tomorrow, Sire.
In his mind's eye, I know, astrologers
are winding suns into his victor's wreath.

(*The* PRINCE *looks the wreath over.*)

THE COURTIER

He's finished now.

HOHENZOLLERN

It is a thousand pities
no looking glass is anywhere nearby:
conceited as a girl, he'd go to it
and try the garland on, this way and that,
as though it were some kind of floral bonnet.

THE ELECTOR

By God, I want to see how far he'll go!

(*The* ELECTOR *takes the wreath from the* PRINCE, *who
looks at him with reddened face. The* ELECTOR *twines*

his necklace around the wreath and gives it to NATALIA. *The* PRINCE *rises quickly. The* ELECTOR *retreats with* NATALIA, *who raises the wreath. The* PRINCE *follows her with outstretched arms.*)

THE PRINCE OF HOMBURG (*whispering*)

Natalia! My beloved! My betrothed!

THE ELECTOR

Away!

HOHENZOLLERN

What did he say, the fool?

THE COURTIER

What was it?

(*They all ascend the ramp.*)

THE PRINCE OF HOMBURG

Frederick! My Sovereign! Father!

HOHENZOLLERN

What the devil!

THE ELECTOR (*retreating*)

Open the gate for me!

THE PRINCE OF HOMBURG

O my dear mother!

HOHENZOLLERN

The madman! He must be —

THE ELECTRESS

Whom calls he that?

THE PRINCE OF HOMBURG (*reaching for the wreath*)

Oh! Dear! Why are you leaving me? Natalia!

(*He snatches a glove off* NATALIA's *hand.*)

HOHENZOLLERN

In heaven's name, what did he snatch?

THE COURTIER

                              The wreath?

NATALIA

No, no.

HOHENZOLLERN (*opening the gate*)

        In here, Sire, quickly! Let the picture
again entirely vanish from his mind.

THE ELECTOR

Back into nothingness, my Prince of Homburg!
Back into nothingness! If you see fit
we'll meet again out on the battleground.
Such things as these are not attained in dreams.
(*All exeunt. The gate slams shut in front of the* PRINCE.
Pause)

SCENE TWO

For a moment the PRINCE OF HOMBURG *stands amazed in
front of the gate. Then, lost in thought, he descends from
the ramp, pressing the glove to his forehead. As soon as he
arrives at the bottom, he looks up toward the gate again.*

SCENE THREE

Enter COUNT HOHENZOLLERN *from below, through a lattice
gate. He is followed by a* PAGE. *The* PRINCE OF HOMBURG.

THE PAGE (*softly*)

Please listen, Count!

COUNT HOHENZOLLERN (*angrily*)

                    Cicada, hush! — What is it?

THE PAGE

I'm here —

HOHENZOLLERN

          Don't wake him with your chirping! — Well?

What is it?

THE PAGE

          Sir, the Elector sends me here.

His orders are: The Prince, when he awakes,

shall not be told a word about the joke

he's played on him this very moment.

HOHENZOLLERN (*softly*)

                              So?

Why don't you lie down in a field of wheat

and get some sleep? I knew that all along.

(*Exit the* PAGE.)

SCENE FOUR

COUNT HOHENZOLLERN. *The* PRINCE OF HOMBURG.

COUNT HOHENZOLLERN (*stepping behind the* PRINCE, *some distance away, while the* PRINCE *continues to look up the ramp*)

Arthur!

(*The* PRINCE *falls to the ground.*)

He's down; a bullet couldn't do it better.
(*He approaches him.*)
I'm curious now what fable he'll invent
to explain to me why he's come here to sleep.
(*He bends over him.*)
Hey, Arthur! Are you mad? What is the matter?
What are you doing at this place at night?

THE PRINCE OF HOMBURG

Why, friend, I —

HOHENZOLLERN

     Well, I must say! On my word!
The cavalry, whose commandant you are,
left on its march an hour ago, and you,
you're lying in the garden here, asleep.

THE PRINCE OF HOMBURG

What cavalry is that?

HOHENZOLLERN

     The Mamelukes! —
Why, as I live and breathe, he knows no longer
he leads the cavalry of Brandenburg!

THE PRINCE OF HOMBURG (*rising*)

My helmet, quick! My armor!

HOHENZOLLERN

        But where are they?

THE PRINCE OF HOMBURG

Why, on the right, the right, Hal; on the stool!

HOHENZOLLERN

Where? On the stool?

THE PRINCE OF HOMBURG

       Yes; there I think I put —

HOHENZOLLERN (*staring at him*)

In that case, take them off the stool again!

THE PRINCE OF HOMBURG

What glove is this?

(*He looks at the glove in his hand.*)

HOHENZOLLERN

How should I know? — (*aside*) Confound it!

He stripped it off the Princess' arm unnoticed.
(*abruptly*) Be off now, quickly! Why delay?

THE PRINCE OF HOMBURG (*throwing the glove away*)

At once!

Hey, Frank! The rogue! I told him he should wake me!

HOHENZOLLERN (*looking at him*)

He's surely raving mad.

THE PRINCE OF HOMBURG

Upon my oath,
I do not know, dear Henry, where I am.

HOHENZOLLERN

In Fehrbellin, you addlepated dreamer,
behind the castle, on a garden walk!

THE PRINCE OF HOMBURG (*aside*)

Would I were swallowed by the night! Again,
unconscious, I've meandered in the moonlight.
(*collecting himself*)
Forgive! I now remember. As you know, the heat
made sleeping very difficult last night.
I slipped into this garden, overtired,
and then, enveloped sweetly by the night,
her blond hair dripping with a lovely scent —

as is the bridegroom by his Persian bride —
I settled in her arms here. — What's the time?

HOHENZOLLERN

Half past eleven.

THE PRINCE OF HOMBURG

And the squadrons gone?

HOHENZOLLERN

Of course. At ten o'clock, as planned. No doubt
the regiment that leads them, Princess Orange,
has reached the heights of Hackelwitz already,
where, facing Wrangel, they're supposed to cover
our army's quiet approach tomorrow morning.

THE PRINCE OF HOMBURG

It's all the same: old Kottwitz is in charge,
and he knows every purpose of this march.
Besides, at two o'clock tomorrow morning
I would have had to return to Fehrbellin,
because we're still to get our orders here.
So I preferred to stay behind in town. —
Come, let us go. — The Elector knows of nothing?

HOHENZOLLERN

No fear! He's long been in his bed, asleep.
(*They are about to go. The* PRINCE *hesitates, turns
around, and picks up the glove.*)

THE PRINCE OF HOMBURG

What a peculiar dream! — A dazzling palace
of gold and silver opened suddenly.
High from its marble ramp came down to me
the persons all who're dear to me:
the Elector and the Electress and the — third —
What is her name?

HOHENZOLLERN

Whose?

THE PRINCE OF HOMBURG (*groping for her name*)

Hers — the one I mean.

The deaf-and-dumb could call her by her name.

HOHENZOLLERN

Miss Platen?

THE PRINCE OF HOMBURG

No, of course not.

HOHENZOLLERN

Miss Ramin?

THE PRINCE OF HOMBURG

No, no, my friend.

HOHENZOLLERN

Miss Bork? Miss Winterfeld?

THE PRINCE OF HOMBURG

No, no! I beg of you! You miss the pearl
but see the ring in which the pearl is set.

HOHENZOLLERN

In heaven's name, say: Can the face be guessed?
What lady do you mean?

THE PRINCE OF HOMBURG

It doesn't matter.

Since I awoke I have forgot the name,
and for the context here it does not matter.

HOHENZOLLERN

Well, then; continue!

THE PRINCE OF HOMBURG

But don't interrupt me! —

And he, the Elector, with the brow of Zeus,
held in his hand a wreath of laurel leaves.

He now steps close in front of me and winds
around the wreath, to inflame my soul completely,
the precious chain he wears around his neck,
and hands it, to be pressed upon my locks —
Henry —

HOHENZOLLERN

To whom?

THE PRINCE OF HOMBURG

O Henry!

HOHENZOLLERN

Well, speak up!

THE PRINCE OF HOMBURG

It was Miss Platen in all likelihood.

HOHENZOLLERN

Miss Platen? Really? Who's in Prussia now?

THE PRINCE OF HOMBURG

Miss Platen. Yes indeed. Or Miss Ramin.

HOHENZOLLERN

What? Miss Ramin? Don't tell me! She, the redhead?
Miss Platen, with her roguish violet eyes —
we know it's she you like.

THE PRINCE OF HOMBURG

It's she I like. —

HOHENZOLLERN

Well, then: you say she handed you the wreath?

THE PRINCE OF HOMBURG

Like glory's genius, now she holds aloft
the wreath of laurel with the dangling chain
as if about to crown a hero's head.
Unutterably moved, I stretch my hands —
I stretch them out to fasten upon the wreath.

I want to lay my body at her feet.
But, as the mist that hovers over valleys
scatters before a hearty breath of air,
so they evade me, climbing up the ramp.
The ramp expands, as I set foot on it,
endlessly high onto the gate of heaven.
I grope now on my right, now on my left,
anxious to lay my hands on one of them.
In vain! The castle opens suddenly,
a bolt of lightning from within engulfs them,
and then the portals noisily shut again.
Only a glove, impetuously, in pursuit
I capture off my lovely specter's arm. —
And now, as I awake, almighty gods,
it is a glove I'm holding in my hand!

HOHENZOLLERN

Upon my oath! And now you think the glove
belongs to her?

THE PRINCE OF HOMBURG

　　　　　To whom?

HOHENZOLLERN

　　　　　　　　Why, to Miss Platen.

THE PRINCE OF HOMBURG

Miss Platen. Yes indeed. Or Miss Ramin.

HOHENZOLLETN (*laughing*)

Humph! Rascal that you are! You and your visions!
Who knows from what delightful rendezvous,
enjoyed here in the flesh and quite awake,
this glove may still be clinging in your hand!

THE PRINCE OF HOMBURG

May still be — ? By my love!

HOHENZOLLERN

                        Oh, devil take it!
Miss Platen, Miss Ramin — What does it matter?
The post for Prussia will be leaving Sunday next:
that is the quickest way for you to learn
if she has lost this glove. — Come, let us go.
It's twelve o'clock. Why stand around and chat?

THE PRINCE OF HOMBURG (*daydreaming*)

You're right there. Off to bed! But tell me first:
The Electress and her niece, are they still staying here —
you know, the beautiful Princess of Orange —
who arrived in our encampment recently?

HOHENZOLLERN

Why do you ask? (*aside*) I do believe the fool —

THE PRINCE OF HOMBURG

Why? I was told to furnish thirty horsemen
to move them from the zone of war again.
I had to ask Ramin to make arrangements.

HOHENZOLLERN

Don't worry! They're long gone. Gone, or will leave at
    once.
At least, all night, quite ready for departure,
Ramin was standing at the castle gates. —
But come! It's twelve o'clock. Before the battle
I still would like to snatch a little rest.
(*exeunt*)

SCENE FIVE

*Fehrbellin. Hall in the castle. Shooting is heard from afar.
Enter the* ELECTRESS *and* PRINCESS NATALIA, *in traveling*

clothes, led by a COURTIER. *They sit down on one side.*
LADIES-IN-WAITING. *Then enter the* ELECTOR, MARSHAL
DÖRFLING, *the* PRINCE OF HOMBURG (*the glove in his
pocket*), COUNT HOHENZOLLERN, COUNT TRUCHSS, COLONEL
HENNINGS, CAPTAIN GOLZ, *and several other* GENERALS,
COLONELS, *and* OTHER OFFICERS.

THE ELECTOR

What is that shooting, Marshal? Is that Götz?

MARSHAL DÖRFLING

Yes, it is Colonel Götz, my Sovereign Lord,
who led with our advance guard yesterday.
He's sent an officer back here to you
to quiet any worries in advance:
a Swedish unit of some thousand men
has moved ahead unto the Hackel Mountains;
nevertheless Götz guarantees these mountains;
he notifies me that you should proceed
as if they had been taken by his vanguard.

THE ELECTOR (*to the* OFFICERS)

The Marshal knows the orders, gentlemen.
Please take your pencils and make note of them!
(*Taking out their tablets, the* OFFICERS *gather around
the* MARSHAL *on one side.*)

THE ELECTOR (*to the* COURTIER)

Ramin is at the entrance with the coach?

THE COURTIER

One moment, Sire: it has been ordered out.

THE ELECTOR (*sitting down on a chair behind the* ELEC-
TRESS *and* NATALIA)

Ramin will be your escort, dear Elisa,
and thirty hardy horsemen under him.

You're leaving for Kalkhuhn's, my chancellor's, castle
at Havelberg, across the Havel river,
beyond the reach of any Swedish troops.

THE ELECTRESS

And has the ferry been restored to service?

THE ELECTOR

At Havelberg? Arrangements have been made.
Besides it will be day before you reach it.
(*pause*)
Natalia, why so quiet, my darling girl?
What ails my child?

PRINCESS NATALIA

      Dear uncle, I'm afraid.

THE ELECTOR

And yet my little daughter's so secure,
she was no safer in her mother's lap.
(*pause*)

THE ELECTRESS

When will we meet again, do you suppose?

THE ELECTOR

If God grants victory — and no doubt He will —
perhaps as soon as in a few days' time.
(*Enter* PAGES *to serve breakfast to the* LADIES. *The* MAR-
SHAL *begins his dictation. The* PRINCE OF HOMBURG,
holding pencil and tablet, stares at the LADIES.)

THE MARSHAL

His Highness' plan of battle, my commanders,
intends the fleeing Swedish army's ruin
by cutting its connection with the bridgehead
which on the river Rhyn protects its rear.
Now, Colonel Hennings —

COLONEL HENNINGS (*writing*)

Here!

THE MARSHAL

Who by the Sovereign's
wish, today

commands the right wing of our combat forces,
by quietly moving forward through the brush
shall try to turn the left wing of the Swedes,
then bravely fling himself between them and the bridges,
and, in conjunction with Count Truchss —
Count Truchss!

COUNT TRUCHSS

Here!

(*He writes.*)

THE MARSHAL

And, in conjunction with Count Truchss —

(*He pauses.*)

who, facing Wrangel, in the meantime on the heights
has occupied positions with his cannon —

TRUCHSS (*writing*)

Positions with his cannon —

THE MARSHAL

Have you got that?

(*continuing*) Attempt to chase the Swedes into the
swamps

that lie behind the right wing of their forces.

A HAIDUK (*entering*)

The coach is waiting at the entrance, Madam.

(*The* LADIES *rise.*)

THE MARSHAL

The Prince of Homburg —

THE ELECTOR (*also rising*)

And Ramin is ready?

THE HAIDUK

He's waiting at the gates, on horseback, Sire.
(*The* ELECTOR *and the* ELECTRESS *and* NATALIA *take leave of each other.*)

TRUCHSS (*writing*)

That lie behind the right wing of their forces.

THE MARSHAL

The Prince of Homburg —
Where is the Prince of Homburg?

COUNT HOHENZOLLERN (*whispering*)

Arthur!

THE PRINCE OF HOMBURG (*with a start*)

Here!

HOHENZOLLERN

You're not yourself!

THE PRINCE OF HOMBURG

What is my Marshal's pleasure?
(*His face reddening, he assumes his pose with pencil and parchment and writes.*)

THE MARSHAL

To whom His Highness, as at Rathenow,
again entrusts the glorious leadership
of all the cavalry of Brandenburg —
(*He pauses.*)
but without prejudice to Colonel Kottwitz,
who will assist the Prince with his advice —
(*aside to* CAPTAIN GOLZ) Is Kottwitz here?

CAPTAIN GOLZ

No, General. As
you see,

I have been delegated in his stead
to hear the battle orders from your mouth.
(*The* PRINCE *again glances at the* LADIES.)

THE MARSHAL (*continuing*)

Takes up positions on the plain at Hackelwitz,
confronting there the right wing of the Swedes,
at ample distance from the cannon fire.

GOLZ (*writing*)

At ample distance from the cannon fire.
(*The* ELECTRESS *ties a scarf around* NATALIA'S *neck.*
NATALIA, *about to put on her gloves, looks around as if
searching for something.*)

THE ELECTOR (*stepping toward her*)

My little girl, what's wrong?

THE ELECTRESS

Is something missing?

NATALIA

I do not know, dear aunt. I think my glove —
(*They all look about.*)

THE ELECTOR (*to the* LADIES-IN-WAITING)

My ladies, would you kindly take a look!

THE ELECTRESS (*to* NATALIA)

You have it, child.

NATALIA

The right one; but the left?

THE ELECTOR

Perhaps it's lying somewhere in your bedroom?

NATALIA

My dear Miss Bork —

THE ELECTOR (*to the* LADY)

                              Quick!

NATALIA

                                        On the mantelpiece!

(*Exit the* LADY-IN-WAITING.)

THE PRINCE OF HOMBURG (*aside*)

Lord of my life! Dare I believe my ears?

(*He takes the glove from his pocket.*)

THE MARSHAL (*looking at his paper*)

At ample distance from the cannon fire.

(*continuing*) The Prince, upon —

THE PRINCE OF HOMBURG

                              She's looking for the
                              glove!

(*He looks now at the glove, now at* NATALIA.)

THE MARSHAL

Upon our Sovereign's positive command —

GOLZ (*writing*)

Upon our Sovereign's positive command —

THE MARSHAL

No matter how the battle may develop,

will not depart from his assigned position —

THE PRINCE OF HOMBURG

I must see quickly if this is the one.

(*He drops the glove together with his handkerchief. He
picks up the handkerchief again but leaves the glove on
the floor, where everyone can see it.*)

THE MARSHAL (*amazed*)

What is the matter, Highness?

HOHENZOLLERN (*whispering*)

Arthur!

THE PRINCE OF HOMBURG

Here!

HOHENZOLLERN

I think
you have gone mad!

THE PRINCE OF HOMBURG

What is my Marshal's pleasure?
(*He takes pencil and tablet again. The* MARSHAL *gives him a brief questioning look. Pause*)

GOLZ (*having written*)

Will not depart from his assigned position —

THE MARSHAL (*continuing*)

Until, harassed by Hennings and by Truchss —

THE PRINCE OF HOMBURG (*aside to* CAPTAIN GOLZ, *while looking at his tablet*)

Who, my dear Golz? What, I?

GOLZ

Yes, you. Who else?

THE PRINCE OF HOMBURG

I shall not move — ?

GOLZ

Indeed!

THE MARSHAL

Well? Have you got that?

THE PRINCE OF HOMBURG (*aloud*)

Will not depart from my assigned position —
(*He writes.*)

THE MARSHAL

Until, harassed by Hennings and by Truchss —
(*He pauses.*)
the left wing of the Swedes, disorganized,
falls on the right, and all their combat forces
stagger and hurry toward the tract of land
where in the marshes, often crossed by ditches,
it is our very plan to cut them up.

THE ELECTOR

Light, pages! May I have your arms, my dear ones?
(*They prepare to leave.*)

THE MARSHAL

Then he will have the trumpets sound the fanfare.

THE ELECTRESS (*as some* OFFICERS *are bowing*)

Goodby! Don't let us keep you, gentlemen!
(*The* MARSHAL, *too, bows.*)

THE ELECTOR (*stopping suddenly*)

Well! Our young lady's glove! Quick! There it lies.

A COURTIER

Where?

THE ELECTOR

       At the Prince's feet, our cousin's.

THE PRINCE OF HOMBURG (*gallantly*)

                     What?

At my feet? Does this glove belong to you?
(*He picks it up and takes it to* NATALIA.)

NATALIA

I thank you, noble Prince.

THE PRINCE OF HOMBURG (*confused*)

                   Is this glove yours?

NATALIA

Yes, it is mine — the one I have been missing.

(*She takes it and puts it on.*)

THE ELECTRESS (*to the* PRINCE *in departing*)

Farewell, farewell! My blessings and good luck!

See that there is a happy, quick reunion!

(*The* ELECTOR *leaves with the* LADIES. LADIES-IN-WAIT-ING, COURTIERS, *and* PAGES *follow.*)

THE PRINCE OF HOMBURG (*thunderstruck for a moment, then turning to the* OFFICERS *with triumphant steps*)

Then he will have the trumpets sound the fanfare!

(*He pretends that he is writing.*)

THE MARSHAL (*looking into his paper*)

Then he will have the trumpets sound the fanfare. —

The Elector, though, to avoid that by mistake

the blow is struck before the proper time —

(*He pauses.*)

GOLZ

The blow is struck before the proper time —

THE PRINCE OF HOMBURG (*aside to* HOHENZOLLERN, *greatly moved*)

Henry!

HOHENZOLLERN (*angrily*)

What is it? Well? What do you want?

THE PRINCE OF HOMBURG

You didn't see?

HOHENZOLLERN

No, nothing. Blast, be quiet!

THE MARSHAL (*continuing*)

Will from his retinue dispatch an officer

to give the Prince, please note, specific orders

to start the attack against the Swedish forces.
Then only will the trumpets sound the fanfare.
(*The* PRINCE *stands daydreaming.*)
Got that?

GOLZ (*writing*)
Then only will the trumpets sound the fanfare.

THE MARSHAL (*raising his voice*)
Your Highness, have you got that?

THE PRINCE OF HOMBURG
                                        Your pardon, Sir?

THE MARSHAL
Have you made note of it?

THE PRINCE OF HOMBURG
                            About the fanfare?

HOHENZOLLERN (*aside to him, angrily, with emphasis*)
Fanfare be damned! Not until he himself —

GOLZ (*similarly*)
Until he sends —

THE PRINCE OF HOMBURG (*interrupting them*)
                Of course. Not until then —
But then he'll have the trumpets sound the fanfare.
(*He writes. Pause*)

THE MARSHAL
Please note this, Baron Golz: With Colonel Kottwitz
himself, if he can make it possible,
I want to speak before the battle starts.

GOLZ (*with meaning*)
I'll tell him so. You may depend on it.
(*pause*)

THE ELECTOR (*returning*)

Well, generals and commanding officers,
the light of day is breaking. Have you finished?

THE MARSHAL

Yes, Sire; it has been done: your plan of action
has duly been announced to your commanders.

THE ELECTOR (*taking hat and gloves*)

To you, Prince Homburg, I advise composure.
Two victories, as you know, you cost me lately
along the Rhine. Keep proper self-control
and don't deprive me of the third today,
which means to me no less than throne and country.
(*to the* OFFICERS) Follow me! — Frank!

A STABLEBOY (*entering*)

Here!

THE ELECTOR

Hurry, my white horse! —
I want to reach the field before the sun.
(*Exit. The* GENERALS, COLONELS, *and* OTHER OFFICERS
follow.)

SCENE SIX

THE PRINCE OF HOMBURG (*stepping to the foreground*)

Now, on your globe, prodigious child of gods,
whose veiling, like a sail, the wind has raised,
draw near! — You've lightly touched my locks, good fortune;
a token did you throw in floating past,

smiling upon me, from your horn of plenty.
Today, elusive one, I'll seek you out;
I'll apprehend you in the field of battle
and empty all your blessing at my feet,
even if sevenfold, with iron chains,
you're fastened to the Swedes' triumphal car!
(*exit*)

ACT TWO

Battlefield near Fehrbellin.
Enter COLONEL KOTTWITZ, COUNT HOHENZOLLERN, CAPTAIN
GOLZ, *and other* OFFICERS, *at the head of the cavalry.*

COLONEL KOTTWITZ (*offstage*)

Cavalry, halt! Halt and dismount!

COUNT HOHENZOLLERN *and* CAPTAIN GOLZ (*entering*)

Halt, halt!

KOTTWITZ

Who'll help me off my horse, friends?

HOHENZOLLERN *and* GOLZ

Here, old man!

(*exeunt*)

KOTTWITZ (*still offstage*)

My thanks to you, sirs. Ugh! A plague upon me!
To each a noble son for your assistance
to do you equal favor when you crumble!
(*He enters, followed by* HOHENZOLLERN, GOLZ, *and*
OTHERS.)
On horseback I feel full of youth. However,
once I dismount a bitter fight begins,
as if my soul and body tore apart.
(*looking around*) Where is the Prince, our Most Serene
Commander?

27

HOHENZOLLERN

He will return at once.

KOTTWITZ

Where is he now?

HOHENZOLLERN

He rode into the village, which you passed,
behind the brush. He will come back at once.

AN OFFICER

I hear he tumbled with his horse at night.

HOHENZOLLERN

I think he did.

KOTTWITZ

He fell?

HOHENZOLLERN (*turning toward him*)

Of no account!

His horse shied at the mill, but, sliding off it,
he did not suffer any harm at all.
It is not worth a particle of worry.

KOTTWITZ (*climbing on a hill*)

A day of beauty, as I live and breathe,
destined by God, lord of the universe,
for more attractive business than a battle!
A reddish sun is gleaming through the clouds,
and joyful feelings, flying with the lark,
climb to the limpid fragrance of the sky.

GOLZ

Did you find Marshal Dörfling?

KOTTWITZ (*stepping to the foreground*)

Curse it, no!

What does His Excellency have in mind?
Am I a bird, an arrow, an idea,

that I can chase through all the battlefield?
I saw the vanguard on the Hackel Heights
and then the rearguard in the Hackel Valley,
but did not find the Marshal. Thereupon,
I came to join my regiment again.

GOLZ

He'll be disturbed: apparently he had
some weighty matter to confide to you.

AN OFFICER

Here comes the Prince, our Most Serene Commander.

SCENE TWO

Enter the PRINCE OF HOMBURG, *a black sling around his
left hand. The others.*

COLONEL KOTTWITZ

Greetings to you, my young and noble Prince!
During the time you spent back in the village
I formed the horsemen on the valley road.
I think you will be satisfied with me.

THE PRINCE OF HOMBURG

Good morning, Kottwitz — and good morning, friends. —
You know that I praise everything you do.

COUNT HOHENZOLLERN

What were you doing in the village, Arthur?
You look so solemn.

THE PRINCE OF HOMBURG

                    I — was in the chapel
that glimmered through the quiet village shrubs.

As we rode past, the bell was being rung
for worship, moving me to join the rest
in prostrate orisons before its altar.

KOTTWITZ

A reverent young gentleman, indeed!
Glory, success, and victory certainly
will crown the work that is begun with prayer.

THE PRINCE OF HOMBURG

I meant to ask you something, Henry —
(*He edges the* COUNT *to the foreground.*)
What was it at the conference overnight
that Dörfling pointed out concerning me?

HOHENZOLLERN

You were abstracted; I did notice it.

THE PRINCE OF HOMBURG

Abstracted or divided — I don't know.
Dictation makes me nervous.

HOHENZOLLERN

                Fortunately
there really wasn't much for you this time.
Hennings and Truchss, who lead our infantry,
were named to attack the Swedes. Your orders are
to stand by with your horsemen in this valley
until you're sent instructions to attack.

THE PRINCE OF HOMBURG (*after a pause of daydreaming*)

A strange occurrence!

HOHENZOLLERN

              What occurrence, Arthur?
(*He looks at him. — The discharge of a cannon is heard.*)

KOTTWITZ

Up with you! On your horses, gentlemen!

It's Hennings, and the battle has begun.
(*They all climb on a hill.*)

THE PRINCE OF HOMBURG

Who is it? What?

HOHENZOLLERN

It's Colonel Hennings, Arthur,
who sneaked around the rear of Wrangel's forces.
Come: from up there you can observe it all.

CAPTAIN GOLZ (*on the hill*)

They're spreading formidably at the Rhyn!

THE PRINCE OF HOMBURG (*shading his eyes*)

What? Hennings on the right?

FIRST OFFICER

Yes, noble Prince.

THE PRINCE OF HOMBURG

Hang! He was on the left wing yesterday!
(*cannon salvos in the distance*)

KOTTWITZ

Confound it! From a dozen fiery mouths
Wrangel is letting loose on Hennings' forces.

FIRST OFFICER

Those Swedish ramparts are the proper thing!

SECOND OFFICER

Yes — reaching to the steeple of the church
located in the village in their rear!
(*gunfire close by*)

GOLZ

That's Truchss.

THE PRINCE OF HOMBURG

It's Truchss?

KOTTWITZ

> Yes, Truchss. Now, from
> the front

he's lending his support to Hennings' troops.

THE PRINCE OF HOMBURG

How is it Truchss is in the center?

(*strong gunfire*)

GOLZ

By God, I think the village is on fire.

THIRD OFFICER

It's burning, on my life!

FIRST OFFICER

> It's burning, burning!

A flame is shooting up along the steeple.

GOLZ

Look at the Swedish couriers flying right and left!

SECOND OFFICER

They're taking off

KOTTWITZ

> Where?

FIRST OFFICER

> On their right wing.

THIRD OFFICER

> Yes!

In whole platoons! Three regiments they are.
It seems they want to reinforce their left.

SECOND OFFICER

Indeed! And mounted troops are moving forward
to cover this maneuver of the right.

HOHENZOLLERN (*laughing*)

Ha, they will surely clear the field again

when they observe us hidden in this valley!
(*musket fire*)

KOTTWITZ

Look, brothers, look!

SECOND OFFICER

You hear it?

FIRST OFFICER

Musket fire!

THIRD OFFICER

They're fighting near the ramparts.

GOLZ

Such artillery thunder
I have not heard in all my living days.

HOHENZOLLERN

Shoot! Shoot and let the ground be cleft asunder!
Then the crevasse shall be your bodies' tomb.
(*Pause. Shouts of victory in the distance*)

FIRST OFFICER

O Lord in heaven, who confers success:
Wrangel is starting to retreat.

HOHENZOLLERN

No, really?

GOLZ

In heaven's name, friends: on the left wing, look!
He's moving from the ramparts with his guns.

ALL

Hurrah, hurrah! Now victory has been won.

THE PRINCE OF HOMBURG (*descending from the hill*)

Come, Kottwitz, follow me!

KOTTWITZ

Be calm, my children!

THE PRINCE OF HOMBURG

Come, have them sound the fanfare! Follow me!

KOTTWITZ

I say again: Be calm!

THE PRINCE OF HOMBURG (*vehemently*)

                 Hell and damnation!

KOTTWITZ

The Elector at the conference overnight
commanded that we wait for special orders.
Golz, read the minutes to the gentleman!

THE PRINCE OF HOMBURG

For orders? Do you ride that slowly, Kottwitz?
Have you not yet received them from your heart?

KOTTWITZ

My orders?

HOHENZOLLERN

        Please!

KOTTWITZ

               Received them from my heart?

HOHENZOLLERN

Please listen to me, Arthur!

GOLZ

              Hear me, Colonel!

KOTTWITZ (*offended*)

Is that the way you talk to me, young sir?
The nag you gallop on I can, if need be,
drag by the tail of mine. — Come, gentlemen!
To battle! Sound the fanfare! I am with you.

GOLZ (*to* **KOTTWITZ**)

No, never, Colonel! In no circumstances!

SECOND OFFICER

The Rhyn has not been reached by Hennings' troops.

FIRST OFFICER

Go, take his saber!

THE PRINCE OF HOMBURG

                    Take my saber? What?

(*He shoves him back.*)

Impertinent stripling, you, who do not know

the ten commandments yet of Brandenburg!

Here is your own, together with the scabbard!

(*He tears off his saber and sabretache.*)

FIRST OFFICER (*tumbling*)

My Prince, this deed! By God!

THE PRINCE OF HOMBURG (*stepping toward him*)

                         Are you still talking?

HOHENZOLLERN (*to the OFFICER*)

Hush! Are you crazy?

THE PRINCE OF HOMBURG (*delivering the saber*)

                    Orderlies,

take him away to Fehrbellin, a prisoner!

(*to KOTTWITZ and the other OFFICERS*)

And now the word is, gentlemen: A scoundrel

who disregards his general's call to battle!

Which of you stays?

KOTTWITZ

                    You heard me. Why the fuss?

HOHENZOLLERN (*appeasing*)

It only was a question of advice.

KOTTWITZ

Take it upon yourself! I follow you.

THE PRINCE OF HOMBURG (*appeased*)
    I take it on myself. Friends, follow me!
    (*exeunt*)

SCENE THREE

Room in a village.
Enter a COURTIER *with boots and spurs. A* FARMER *and his*
WIFE *are sitting at a table, working.*

THE COURTIER
    Good morning, my good people! Have you room
    to put up guests in your establishment?

THE FARMER
    Why, yes. With pleasure.

THE FARMER'S WIFE
                                Will you tell us whom?

THE COURTIER
    The foremost lady of the land, none less.
    The axle of her coach broke at the gate,
    and as we hear that victory has been won,
    the journey is no longer necessary.

THE FARMER *and his* WIFE (*rising*)
    A victory won? Good heavens!

THE COURTIER
                                Don't you know?
    The Swedish army has been soundly beaten,
    and from its fire and sword the march is safe,
    if not forever, for a year's duration. —
    But look: here comes the lady of the land.

SCENE FOUR

Enter the ELECTRESS, *pale and distraught, followed by* PRINCESS NATALIA *and several* LADIES-IN-WAITING. *The others.*

THE ELECTRESS (*on the threshold*)

Miss Bork, Miss Winterfeld, give me your arms!

PRINCESS NATALIA (*hurrying to her*)

O my dear mother!

THE LADIES-IN-WAITING

God, she pales, she's fainting.

(*They support her.*)

THE ELECTRESS

I want to sit down. Lead me to a chair!

Dead, he says? Dead?

NATALIA

O my beloved mother!

THE ELECTRESS

I want to see that envoy of misfortune.

SCENE FIVE

Enter CAPTAIN MÖRNER, *wounded, led by two* HORSEMEN. *The others.*

THE ELECTRESS

What do you bring me, bearer of dread tidings?

CAPTAIN MÖRNER

Alas, what, to my everlasting sorrow,

I saw with my own eyes, beloved lady.

THE ELECTRESS

Give your report!

MÖRNER

The Elector is no more.

PRINCESS NATALIA

Dear heaven!

Are we to suffer such an awful blow?
(*She covers her face.*)

THE ELECTRESS

Render me your report on how he fell.
Before the lightning hits the wanderer,
it lights his world once more in purple colors:
thus shall your speech; and then, when you have spoken,
may dark of night descend upon my head!

MÖRNER (*stepping before her, led by the two* HORSEMEN)

As soon as, pressed by Truchss, the Swedish troops
had started giving way, the Prince of Homburg
moved forward against Wrangel on the plain.
Two lines his cavalry had penetrated
and then annihilated in pursuit
when it was halted by a field redoubt.
Met there by deadly rain of iron, his horsemen
buckled and flattened like a crop of wheat.
Between the brush and hills he had to stop
to re-collect his scattered horsemen's corps.

NATALIA (*to the* ELECTRESS)

Courage, beloved!

THE ELECTRESS

Let me be, my dear!

MÖRNER

That moment, having left the dust behind us,

we see the Elector riding with the standards
of Truchss's corps against the Swedish forces.
Upon a white horse, a majestic sight,
he lit the path of victory in the sun.
On seeing this, we gather on a slope,
perturbed to know him in the thick of fire,
when suddenly the Sovereign, horse and horseman,
sinks to the ground before our very eyes.
Two standard bearers, falling over him,
cover him with their standards.

NATALIA

       My dear mother!

FIRST LADY-IN-WAITING

Heavens!

THE ELECTRESS

    Go on, go on!

MÖRNER

       This dreadful sight
fills with immense distress the Prince's heart,
and, spurred to vengeful fury, like a bear,
he flings himself with us against the rampart.
We fly across the ditch and parapet;
the garrison is defeated, scattered, killed;
cannons and standards, flags and kettledrums,
all of the baggage of the Swedes are captured.
And had the bridgehead on the Rhyn not checked us
in our destruction, no one would be left
to utter at the homestead of his fathers:
I saw the hero fall at Fehrbellin.

THE ELECTRESS

A victory bought too dearly! I don't want it.

Return to me the price we've paid for it!
(*She faints.*)

FIRST LADY-IN-WAITING

Help us, O Lord! She's losing consciousness.
(NATALIA *cries.*)

SCENE SIX

Enter THE PRINCE OF HOMBURG. *The others.*

THE PRINCE OF HOMBURG

My dear Natalia!
(*Greatly moved, he puts her hand to his heart.*)

PRINCESS NATALIA

Is it really true?

THE PRINCE OF HOMBURG

If only I could say that it was not!
If only with the blood of this true heart
I could call his back to reality!

NATALIA (*drying her tears*)

Have they then found the body?

THE PRINCE OF HOMBURG

Until now
my only task has been revenge on Wrangel;
how could I set my mind upon such care?
I have, however, sent a group of men
to find him on the field of death. No doubt
he will arrive here still before tonight.

NATALIA

Who'll check those Swedes now in this awful struggle?

Who will protect us from this world of foes,
supplied us by his fortune and his glory?

THE PRINCE OF HOMBURG (*taking her hand*)

I'll stand, an angel with a flaming sword,
beside your orphaned throne. The Elector wanted
to see the marches freed before year's end;
I'll be the executor of that last will.

NATALIA

My dear, my cherished cousin!
(*She withdraws her hand.*)

THE PRINCE OF HOMBURG

                              Dear Natalia!

(*He pauses for a moment.*)
What do you think about your future now?

NATALIA

What shall I do now that this thunderbolt
has torn apart the ground beneath my feet?
My father, my dear mother are at rest
in Amsterdam. Our patrimony, Dordrecht,
lies ruined. Pressed by Spanish tyrant's armies,
my cousin Maurice of Orange barely knows
where his own children might be safe. And now
this last prop of my fortune's vine is falling.
Today I'm orphaned for the second time.

THE PRINCE OF HOMBURG (*putting his arm around her*)

My dear girl, were this hour not dedicated
to mourning, I would want to say to you:
Entwine your branches here around this breast!
For years, in lonely bloom, it has been wanting
the lovely scent of your campanulas.

NATALIA

My excellent, cherished cousin!

THE PRINCE OF HOMBURG

Would you, would you?

NATALIA

If I may grow into its inner mark?
(*She leans against his breast.*)

THE PRINCE OF HOMBURG

What? How was that?

NATALIA

Away!

THE PRINCE OF HOMBURG (*holding her*)

Into its core!

Into its very heart, Natalia!
(*He kisses her. She tears herself away.*)

God!

Would he were here now whom we are lamenting
to witness this our covenant! Would we could
stammer to him: O father, give your blessing!
(*He covers his face with his hands.* NATALIA *turns back
toward the* ELECTRESS.)

SCENE SEVEN

A SERGEANT MAJOR *rushes in. The others.*

THE SERGEANT MAJOR

My Prince, I dare not, by the living God,
report to you the rumor that is spreading:
the Elector is alive!

THE PRINCE OF HOMBURG
                    Alive?

THE SERGEANT MAJOR
                         By heaven!
Count Sparren has just come here with this news.

PRINCESS NATALIA
Lord of my life! O mother, do you hear?
(*She sinks down before the* ELECTRESS *and embraces
her.*)

THE PRINCE OF HOMBURG
No, tell me — Who has brought — ?

THE SERGEANT MAJOR
                              Count George of Sparren,
who saw him safe and sound with his own eyes
at Hackelwitz with Truchss's corps.

THE PRINCE OF HOMBURG
                         Be quick,
old fellow! Run and bring him here to me!
(*Exit the* SERGEANT MAJOR.)

SCENE EIGHT

Enter COUNT GEORGE OF SPARREN *and the* SERGEANT MAJOR.
The others.

THE ELECTRESS
Oh, do not fling me twice into the abyss!

PRINCESS NATALIA
No, my dear mother.

THE ELECTRESS

     Frederick is alive?

NATALIA (*supporting her with both hands*)

 You enjoy supreme existence once again.

THE SERGEANT MAJOR (*entering*)

 Here is the captain now, Sir.

THE PRINCE OF HOMBURG

      Count of Sparren,

 you have beheld the Sovereign, safe and sound,

 with Truchss's corps at Hackelwitz?

COUNT OF SPARREN

        I have,

 my noble Prince. There, in the parson's yard,

 surrounded by his staff, he issued orders

 for burial of the dead of either side.

THE LADIES-IN-WAITING (*embracing one another*)

 O God!

THE ELECTRESS

   Dear girl!

NATALIA

     This bliss is overwhelming.

 (*She presses her face into the* ELECTRESS' *lap.*)

THE PRINCE OF HOMBURG

 Did I not, with my horsemen, from afar

 catch sight of him as, smashed by cannon balls,

 he and his white horse sank into the dust?

SPARREN

 Indeed, the white horse, with its rider, fell,

 but, Prince, the Sovereign was not riding it.

THE PRINCE OF HOMBURG

 No? Not the Sovereign?

NATALIA

Wonderful!

(*She rises and steps to the* ELECTRESS' *side.*)

THE PRINCE OF HOMBURG

Speak! Tell!

Heavy as gold your words weigh in my heart.

SPARREN

Let me report the most pathetic story
that ever came to anybody's ears. —
The Sovereign, deaf to caution, rode again
the radiantly white horse which recently
Equerry Froben bought for him in England.
Again he was, as always to this day,
the target of the hostile cannon balls.
His train was barely able to approach
within a radius of a hundred paces.
Grenades as well as cannon balls and grapeshot
rolled toward him like a broad stream of destruction,
and everything alive made for the shore;
but he, the daring swimmer, did not swerve,
and, always waving to his friends, he swam
undaunted toward the river's source above.

THE PRINCE OF HOMBURG

By heaven, yes: it was a dreadful sight.

COUNT SPARREN

Equerry Froben, nearest in his train,
calls to me with these words: "Accursed be
today the luster of this horse, which lately
I bought in London for a pot of gold!
I'd give the sum of fifty ducats now
if I could mask it with the gray of mice."

He nears him full of fervent care and says:
"Your horse is skittish, Highness. Please permit
to put it through its paces once again!"
And with these words, alighting from his chestnut,
he grabs the bridle of the Sovereign's beast.
Dismounting with a smile, the Sovereign answers:
"The art that you would teach it, my old man,
it surely will not master during daytime.
Please take it far away behind those hills,
for there the Swedish will not heed its fault."
And thereupon he climbs on Froben's chestnut
and rides back where his duty summons him.
But Froben has no sooner climbed his mount
than both he and the horse are beaten down
by deadly lead sent from the field redoubt.
He falls a victim of his loyalty,
and not another sound was heard from him.
(*short pause*)

THE PRINCE OF HOMBURG

He has been paid. Had I ten lives to spend,
I could not use them better than he did.

NATALIA

O honorable Froben!

THE ELECTRESS

Excellent man!

NATALIA

A lesser man would be worth weeping over.
(*They cry.*)

THE PRINCE OF HOMBURG

Please! To the point: where is the Elector now?
Has he moved on to Hackelwitz?

SPARREN

No, Sir.
The Sovereign has departed for Berlin,
and all of our commanding officers
have been requested there to follow him.

THE PRINCE OF HOMBURG

What? To Berlin? Hostilities are over?

SPARREN

I am amazed all this is news to you.
The Swedish general Count of Horn has come,
and in the encampment after his arrival
an armistice was presently proclaimed.
If I have rightly understood the Marshal,
negotiations have begun. It's possible
that peace itself may be the consequence.

THE ELECTRESS

God, how sublimely everything is clearing!
(*She rises.*)

THE PRINCE OF HOMBURG

Come, let us follow to Berlin at once. —
Would you be kind enough, for quicker transport,
to grant a seat to me in your conveyance? —
Let me just write a line or two to Kottwitz,
and then I'll board the coach with you at once.
(*He sits down and writes.*)

THE ELECTRESS

Why, certainly; with pleasure.
(*The* PRINCE *folds his letter and gives it to the* SERGEANT
MAJOR. *Then he again turns to the* ELECTRESS *and gently
puts an arm around* NATALIA.)

THE PRINCE OF HOMBURG

It so happens
I have a wish to impart to you in quiet.
I'll talk to you about it on the journey.

NATALIA (*breaking away from him*)

Quickly, Miss Bork, my kerchief!

THE ELECTRESS

You, a wish?

FIRST LADY-IN-WAITING

You're wearing it around your neck, Princess.

THE PRINCE OF HOMBURG (*to the* ELECTRESS)

You cannot guess?

THE ELECTRESS

No, nothing.

THE PRINCE OF HOMBURG

Not a word?

THE ELECTRESS (*cutting him short*)

Today, however, I would not deny
the suit of any suppliant on this earth,
least of all yours, the victor's in the battle. —
Let us be off!

THE PRINCE OF HOMBURG

What did you say, dear mother?
May I construe your words as I see fit?

THE ELECTRESS

Let us be off, I say. More in the coach!
Come, let me have your arm.

THE PRINCE OF HOMBURG

O Caesar Divus,
the ladder now I lay against your star!

(*He leads the* LADIES *away. The others follow.*)

SCENE NINE

*Berlin. Park in front of the old castle. In the background
the castle church, with steps. Ringing of bells. The church
is fully lighted.* FROBEN's *body is carried past and is set on
a magnificent catafalque.*

Enter the ELECTOR, MARSHAL DÖRFLING, COLONEL HEN-
NINGS, COUNT TRUCHSS, *and several other* COLONELS *and*
OTHER OFFICERS. *On the opposite side, enter several* OFFI-
CERS *with dispatches.* PEOPLE OF ALL AGES *in the church
and on the square.*

THE ELECTOR

No matter who was in command that day
and, self-willed, launched the horsemen on their charge
before I gave the word compelling him,
and Colonel Hennings having been unable
to wreck the enemy bridges — he, I say,
is guilty of a crime deserving death
and shall be tried by military court. —
The Prince of Homburg was not in command?

COUNT TRUCHSS

No, he was not, Sire.

THE ELECTOR

                                    Who informs me so?

TRUCHSS

Some of the horsemen can corroborate it
who told me so before the battle started:
the Prince received some serious injuries
on head and thighs when falling with his horse;
his wounds were bandaged in a church.

THE ELECTOR

No matter. —

The victory has been brilliant, and tomorrow
I'll offer thanks to God before the altar;
but ten times greater, it would not excuse
him through whom chance awarded it to me.
More battles yet than this one I must fight,
and I demand obedience to the law.
Whoever it was who led them into battle
has forfeited his head, I say again,
and shall appear in military court. —
Come, friends, and follow me into the church!

SCENE TEN

Enter the PRINCE OF HOMBURG, *holding three Swedish
flags;* COLONEL KOTTWITZ, *holding two; and* COUNT HOHEN-
ZOLLERN, CAPTAIN GOLZ, *and* COUNT REUSS, *each holding
one. Several other* OFFICERS, CORPORALS, *and* HORSEMEN,
with flags, kettledrums, and standards. The others.
MARSHAL DÖRFLING (*seeing the* PRINCE)

The Prince of Homburg! Truchss, what did you do?
THE ELECTOR (*with a start*)

Where are you coming from, Prince?
THE PRINCE OF HOMBURG (*taking a few steps forward*)

Fehrbellin, my Sov-
ereign.

These victory trophies I have brought for you.
(*He places three flags at his feet. The* OFFICERS, COR-
PORALS, *and* HORSEMEN *follow suit.*)

THE ELECTOR (*taken aback*)

    I understand you're wounded — seriously?

    Count Truchss?

THE PRINCE OF HOMBURG

            Indeed?

COUNT TRUCHSS

               By heaven, I'm amazed.

THE PRINCE OF HOMBURG

    My chestnut fell before the battle started.

    This hand here, bandaged by an army surgeon,

    does not deserve to be described as wounded.

THE ELECTOR

    Then it was you who led the cavalry?

THE PRINCE OF HOMBURG (*looking him in the eye*)

    I? Yes indeed. Am I the one to tell you?

    The proof I've just deposited before you.

THE ELECTOR

    Divest him of his saber: he's a prisoner.

THE MARSHAL (*aghast*)

    Whose saber?

THE ELECTOR (*stepping among the flags*)

          Kottwitz, how are you?

TRUCHSS (*aside*)

                  Oh damn!

COLONEL KOTTWITZ

    By God, I'm utterly —

THE ELECTOR (*looking at him*)

            What did you say? —

    Look, what a harvest reaped for our renown!

    This is the Swedish Guardsmen's, is it not?

    (*He picks up the flag, unfurls it, and looks at it.*)

KOTTWITZ

My Lord?

THE MARSHAL

My Sovereign?

THE ELECTOR

Yes, indeed it is.
And from King Gustaf Adolf's times at that!
What's the inscription?

KOTTWITZ

I think —

THE MARSHAL

Per aspera ad astra.

THE ELECTOR

That pledge it did not keep at Fehrbellin.
(*pause*)

KOTTWITZ (*timidly*)

Sire, may I say a word?

THE ELECTOR

I beg your pardon? —
Take all, the flags and kettledrums and standards,
and hang them on the pillars of the church!
I mean to use them at the fête tomorrow.
(*The* ELECTOR *turns to the couriers. He takes their dispatches, opens them, and reads them.*)

KOTTWITZ

That, by the living God, I find too much!
(*After some hesitation,* KOTTWITZ *picks up his two flags. The other* OFFICERS *and* HORSEMEN *follow suit. Finally, as the* PRINCE OF HOMBURG's *three flags remain on the ground,* KOTTWITZ *picks them up, too, and is now carrying five.*)

AN OFFICER (*stepping toward the* PRINCE)

Prince, may I have your saber?

COUNT HOHENZOLLERN (*joining the* PRINCE *with his flag*)

Quiet, friend!

THE PRINCE OF HOMBURG

Am I awake or dreaming? Living? Conscious?

CAPTAIN GOLZ

Prince, I would give the saber and be quiet.

THE PRINCE OF HOMBURG

I am a prisoner?

HOHENZOLLERN

So you are.

GOLZ

You've heard.

THE PRINCE OF HOMBURG

And may one know the reason?

HOHENZOLLERN (*with emphasis*)

No, not now.

You pushed into the battle prematurely,

just as we told you then; your orders were

not to give up your post without command.

THE PRINCE OF HOMBURG

Help me, friends, help! I've gone insane.

GOLZ (*interrupting*)

Be still!

THE PRINCE OF HOMBURG

Have then the Brandenburgers been defeated?

HOHENZOLLERN (*stamping his foot*)

No matter. Regulations must prevail.

THE PRINCE OF HOMBURG (*with bitterness*)

So! — So, so, so!

HOHENZOLLERN (*walking away*)

        It will not cost your neck.

GOLZ (*also walking away*)

Perhaps you will be free again tomorrow.

(*The* ELECTOR *folds the letters again and returns to the* OFFICERS.)

THE PRINCE OF HOMBURG (*after taking off his saber*)

My cousin Frederick wants to pose as Brutus!
He sees himself, in colors drawn on canvas,
already sitting on the curule chair,
the Swedish standards lying in the foreground,
the march's code of war upon the table.
By God, in me he will not find the son
to sound his praises on the headsman's block!
I'm wont to find a good old German heart,
a heart of generosity and love;
and if he does approach me at this moment
with all the rigor of antiquity,
I'm sorry for him and must pity him.

(*Exit after surrendering his saber to the* OFFICER.)

THE ELECTOR

Take him to Fehrbellin and summon there
the military court to hear his case!

(*Exit into the church. While he and his retinue are kneeling for prayer at* FROBEN's *coffin, the flags are hung on the pillars of the church. Funeral music.*)

ACT THREE

Fehrbellin. A prison.
The PRINCE OF HOMBURG. *In the background two* HORSE-
MEN *as guards. Enter* COUNT HOHENZOLLERN.

THE PRINCE OF HOMBURG

Henry, my friend! I'm glad to see you. Welcome. –
Well, now: I'm rid of the imprisonment?

COUNT HOHENZOLLERN (*surprised*)

The Lord above be praised!

THE PRINCE OF HOMBURG

                    I beg your pardon?

HOHENZOLLERN

You're rid of it? He's sent you back your saber?

THE PRINCE OF HOMBURG

Me?

HOHENZOLLERN

     Has he not?

THE PRINCE OF HOMBURG

          No!

HOHENZOLLERN

         How then rid of it?

THE PRINCE OF HOMBURG (*after a pause*)

I thought you came to tell me. Never mind!

HOHENZOLLERN

I know of nothing.

THE PRINCE OF HOMBURG

Never mind, I say.

He will send someone else to tell me so.

(*He turns and gets some chairs.*)

Sit down! — Well, come and tell me all the news!

The Elector has returned here from Berlin?

HOHENZOLLERN (*absentminded*)

Last night, yes.

THE PRINCE OF HOMBURG

And the victory celebration —

did it come off as planned? — Why, yes; of course. —

And was the Elector present in the church?

HOHENZOLLERN

He was; the Electress and Natalia, too.

The church was lighted in a stately manner,

and guns were sounding from the castle square

in solemn splendor during the Te Deum.

The flags and standards of the Swedes were flying

as trophies from the pillars, and your name,

upon the Sovereign's strict instructions,

was mentioned from the pulpit as the victor's.

THE PRINCE OF HOMBURG

So I have heard. — Well, is there other news?

It seems to me you don't look cheerful, friend.

HOHENZOLLERN

Have you had word with anyone?

THE PRINCE OF HOMBURG

                    With Golz:

after the trial I saw him at the castle.

(*pause*)

HOHENZOLLERN (*looking at him anxiously*)

What do you think of your position, Arthur,
following all these strange developments?

THE PRINCE OF HOMBURG

The same as you and Golz — the court itself!
The Elector acted as his duty bade him,
and now he'll listen to his heart as well.
"You've blundered," he will tell me seriously —
then drop a word perhaps of death and fortress —
"but now receive your liberty again!"
Around the sword that gained the victory for him
perhaps is wound some ornament of mercy —
If not, all right; that I did not deserve.

HOHENZOLLERN

O Arthur!

(*He pauses.*)

THE PRINCE OF HOMBURG

           Well?

HOHENZOLLERN

                You are so sure of that?

THE PRINCE OF HOMBURG

That's how I picture it! I know he loves me
as if I were his son; his heart has proved it
a thousand times to me since early childhood.
What reason do you have for being doubtful?
Did he not watch my youthful glory grow
with almost greater joy than I myself?

Am I not everything I am through him?
And he, he should, devoid of love and care,
now want to crush into the dust the plant
that he himself raised just because it bloomed
a bit too quickly and luxuriantly?
His greatest foe could not convince me of it;
much less can you, who know and cherish him.

HOHENZOLLERN (*with meaning*)

Arthur, you've faced the military court
and think so still?

THE PRINCE OF HOMBURG

Yes; for that very reason!
No one, by God, would go as far as this
who did not contemplate to grant a pardon!
Just there it was, there at the bar of judgment,
that I attained my confidence again.
Was it a crime deserving death, I ask you,
to thrust the Swedish might into the dust
two moments sooner than it had been ordered?
What other trespass am I guilty of?
How could he summon me before that bench
of heartless judges, singing me like owls
the funeral chant about the firing squad,
unless, serenely, with a ruler's verdict
he meant to step among them like a god?
No, friend: in gathering now this night of clouds
about my head, he merely contemplates
to pierce their misty sphere, a radiant sun;
and that delight I really cannot grudge him.

HOHENZOLLERN

And yet they say the court has passed its sentence.

THE PRINCE OF HOMBURG

So I have heard: for death.

HOHENZOLLERN (*surprised*)

You know about it?

THE PRINCE OF HOMBURG

Golz, who was present when it passed the sentence,
told me about the outcome.

HOHENZOLLERN

Well, by God!

That does not move you?

THE PRINCE OF HOMBURG

Not at all.

HOHENZOLLERN

You're mad!

What is the basis of your confidence?

THE PRINCE OF HOMBURG

My intuition of him.
(*He rises.*)

Let me be!
Why should I labor under groundless doubts?
(*He collects his thoughts and sits down again. Pause*)
The judges' sentence had to be for death;
so says the law that guides their judgment. Yet,
before he'd have such sentence executed,
before he'd yield this heart, which loves him truly,
by sign of kerchief, to a rifle shot,
he'd rather open his own breast, you see,
and drip his blood himself into the dust.

HOHENZOLLERN

Now, Arthur, I assure you —

THE PRINCE OF HOMBURG (*annoyed*)
>Henry, please!

HOHENZOLLERN
>The Marshal —

THE PRINCE OF HOMBURG (*still annoyed*)
>Let me be!

HOHENZOLLERN
>Just two more words!
>If they mean nothing either, I'll be silent.

THE PRINCE OF HOMBURG (*turning toward him again*)
>You hear: I know of everything. — What is it?

HOHENZOLLERN
>It's very strange: a while ago, the Marshal
>went to present the sentence at the castle;
>and he, instead of granting you a pardon —
>an option which is left him by the sentence —
>asked that it come to him for signature.

THE PRINCE OF HOMBURG
>All right, I say.

HOHENZOLLERN
>All right?

THE PRINCE OF HOMBURG
>For signature?

HOHENZOLLERN
>I can assure you; on my word of honor!

THE PRINCE OF HOMBURG
>The sentence? — No! — The writ?

HOHENZOLLERN
>The capital sentence.

THE PRINCE OF HOMBURG
>Who's told you that?

HOHENZOLLERN

> The Marshal; he himself.

THE PRINCE OF HOMBURG
When?

HOHENZOLLERN

> Just this moment.

THE PRINCE OF HOMBURG

> > Having seen the Sovereign?

HOHENZOLLERN
As he was coming down the stairs from him.
Observing how perturbed I was, he added
that all was not yet lost and that tomorrow
was still another day to pardon you.
His pallid lips denied their very words;
they seemed to say: There's little likelihood.

THE PRINCE OF HOMBURG (*rising*)
Might he be — no! — might he be turning over
such monstrous resolutions in his heart?
Crush underfoot the giver of the diamond
he just received because it has a flaw
that even glasses barely can detect?
A deed that would burn white the Dey of Algiers,
adorn with cherub's wings of shining silver
King Sardanapalus, and as innocent
throw to the right of God all Roman tyrants,
like infants dying at their mothers' breasts?

HOHENZOLLERN (*also having risen*)
You must resolve all doubt about that, friend.

THE PRINCE OF HOMBURG
The Marshal, then, was silent and said nothing?

HOHENZOLLERN

What should he say?

THE PRINCE OF HOMBURG

Dear heaven! All my hopes!

HOHENZOLLERN

Have you at any time done anything,
on purpose or unwittingly,
to trench upon his pride?

THE PRINCE OF HOMBURG

No, never!

HOHENZOLLERN

Think!

THE PRINCE OF HOMBURG

By heaven, no! The shadow of his head
was sacred to me.

HOHENZOLLERN

Arthur, don't be angry
if I have doubts. The Ambassador of Sweden,
Count Horn, arrived; the subject of his mission
is said to be Natalia, Princess Orange.
A few words uttered by your aunt, the Electress,
have jarred the Sovereign grievously. They say
the Princess has already made her choice.
Are you involved in this in any way?

THE PRINCE OF HOMBURG

O God! What are you saying?

HOHENZOLLERN

Are you? Are you?

THE PRINCE OF HOMBURG

I am, my friend; now all is clear to me.
My proposition to her ruins me:

I am responsible for her refusal,

because the Princess promised to be mine.

HOHENZOLLERN

You inconsiderate fool! What have you done?

How often have I warned you as a friend!

THE PRINCE OF HOMBURG

Henry, I'm lost! Please help me, rescue me!

HOHENZOLLERN

But what deliverance is there from these straits? —

Perhaps you ought to see your aunt, the Electress?

THE PRINCE OF HOMBURG (*turning*)

Hey, sentry!

A HORSEMAN (*in the background*)

        Here, Sir!

THE PRINCE OF HOMBURG

        Call your officer!

(*He hurriedly takes a cloak from the wall, drapes it around himself, and puts on the hat which has been lying on the table.*)

HOHENZOLLERN (*helping him*)

Turned to account, this step may bring salvation;

for if the Elector can conclude a peace

with King Karl for that certain price, you'll see:

His heart will reconcile itself with you

and you'll be free again in several hours.

SCENE TWO

Enter an OFFICER. *The others.*

THE PRINCE OF HOMBURG (*to the* OFFICER)

Stranz, I'm detained here in your custody.

Permit me to be absent for an hour
on urgent business.

THE OFFICER

                    Prince, you're not detained:
the instructions I've been given indicate
you're free to go wherever you desire.

THE PRINCE OF HOMBURG

Remarkable! I'm not a prisoner, then?

THE OFFICER

Your pardon, Sir: you're fettered by your word.

THE PRINCE OF HOMBURG (*leaving*)

All right too! Never mind! — Goodby, my friend!

HOHENZOLLERN

The fetters follow in the Prince's trail!

THE PRINCE OF HOMBURG

I'm off to see my aunt up at the castle.
I will be back again in just a moment.
(*exeunt*)

SCENE THREE

Chamber of the ELECTRESS. *Enter the* ELECTRESS *and* PRINCESS NATALIA.

THE ELECTRESS

Come, my dear daughter, come, your hour is here.
Count Gustaf Horn, the Ambassador of Sweden,
and all the other guests have left the castle.
I see there's light up in your uncle's chamber.

Come, take your scarf, go to him silently,
and see what you can do to save your friend!
(*They are about to go.*)

SCENE FOUR

Enter a LADY-IN-WAITING. *The others.*

THE LADY-IN-WAITING

Madam, the Prince of Homburg is outside!
I hardly know if I can trust my eyes.

THE ELECTRESS (*taken aback*)

God!

PRINCESS NATALIA

He himself?

THE ELECTRESS

He's not in custody?

THE LADY-IN-WAITING

He's standing at the door with hat and coat,
upset and anxious, begging to be heard.

THE ELECTRESS (*annoyed*)

How rash of him that he should break his word!

PRINCESS NATALIA

Who knows what's troubling him?

THE ELECTRESS (*after some hesitation*)

Let him come in.

(*She sits down on a chair.*)

SCENE FIVE

Enter the PRINCE OF HOMBURG. *The others.*

THE PRINCE OF HOMBURG

   O my dear mother!
   (*He falls on his knees.*)

THE ELECTRESS

                Prince, what brings you here?

THE PRINCE OF HOMBURG

   Let me embrace your knees, dear mother!

THE ELECTRESS

                            Prince,

   although a prisoner, you've come here to see us.
   Why are you adding to your other guilt?

THE PRINCE OF HOMBURG (*anxious*)

   You know what they have done?

THE ELECTRESS

                     Yes, I know all.

   But how can I, poor soul, lend you support?

THE PRINCE OF HOMBURG

   You would not speak thus, mother, if like me
   you felt the shiver of death about your person.
   You and the Princess and your ladies, all
   appear endowed with heaven's saving powers.
   I could embrace your lowest stableboy,
   who tends your horses, begging him to save me.
   I am the only one in all creation
   without support, deserted, powerless.

THE ELECTRESS

   You're quite beside yourself. What has occurred?

THE PRINCE OF HOMBURG

Oh, on the way that led me here to you
I noticed torches, saw them dig the grave
to which my bones shall be consigned tomorrow.
These eyes, aunt, that are gazing on you now,
they want to shroud in darkness; and this breast,
they mean to penetrate with deadly bullets.
Reserved already are the market windows
that look upon the dreary spectacle,
and who today, upon life's pinnacle,
still views the future like a fairyland
will rot between two narrow boards tomorrow,
a tombstone telling you: He was!
(PRINCESS NATALIA, *who at a distance has been leaning on
the shoulder of the* LADY-IN-WAITING, *sits down at a table,
overcome with emotion, and cries.*)

THE ELECTRESS

My son,
if this is what a higher will ordains,
you'll arm yourself with courage and restraint.

THE PRINCE OF HOMBURG

O mother, God's world is so beautiful!
Before my hour arrives, I beg of you,
let me not join those somber shades below!
If I've done wrong and he must punish me,
why must it be the bullet of all things?
Let him relieve me of my offices,
cashier me, if that is the law. — Great God!
I've seen my grave and only want to live;
I do not care for glory any more.

THE ELECTRESS (*with suppressed emotion*)

Get up, my son, get up! What are you saying?
You're overly distraught. Compose yourself!

THE PRINCE OF HOMBURG

No, not before you've promised me, dear aunt,
to entreat him on your knees to spare my life. —
Hedwig, your friend from childhood, on her deathbed,
entrusted me to you at Homburg, saying:
"When I'm no longer, may you be his mother!"
You, kneeling at her bedside, deeply moved,
bent down upon her hand and answered her:
"I shall regard him as my son." — Go, aunt —
remembering now the pledge you uttered then —
as if I were your son and say to him:
"Be merciful, I pray; let him be free!"
And then come back to me and say: "You are."

THE ELECTRESS (*crying*)

O my dear son, it has been done already.
However, all my pleading was in vain.

THE PRINCE OF HOMBURG

I give up any claim to happiness.
As to Natalia, don't forget to tell him,
I yearn for her no longer; in my heart
all tenderness for her has disappeared.
She's free again, as is the doe afield;
she may, as if I never had existed,
betroth herself, and if it is Karl Gustaf,
the Swedish King, I will applaud her for it.
I'll go to my possessions on the Rhine.
I'll build in sweat, pull down, and sow and reap,
as if for wife and child, consume alone,

and, having harvested, I'll sow anew,
and thus will chase my life around in circles
till, dropping in the evening, it expires.

THE ELECTRESS

All right! Return to your imprisonment!
That is the first condition of my favor.

THE PRINCE OF HOMBURG (*rising and turning to* NATALIA)

You're crying, my poor girl! The sun today
is lighting all your hopes the way to death.
Your first emotion centered on my person,
and now your face informs me, true as gold,
that no one else will ever have your love.
What can I, poor soul, do to comfort you?
Go to the convent on the Main, I counsel,
to join your cousin Thurn; there, in the mountains,
look for a boy with locks as fair as mine;
then purchase him with gold and silver, press him
close to your breast, teach him to stammer "mother!"
Later, when he has grown, explain to him
how one should close a dying person's eyes!
That's all the happiness in store for you.

PRINCESS NATALIA (*bravely and encouragingly, rises and
and puts her hand in his*)

Go back to your imprisonment, young hero,
and on your way there quietly once again
look at the grave that's being opened for you!
It gapes no wider nor is any darker
than you've beheld it scores of times in battle.
I, meanwhile, faithful to you unto death,
will venture a word with Uncle in your behalf.
Perhaps I will succeed in moving him

and in delivering you from all misfortune.

(*pause*)

THE PRINCE OF HOMBURG (*folding his hands and gazing at her*)

Had you two wings, my maiden, on your shoulders,
for an angel truly would I take you. God!
Can I believe my ears? You'll speak for me?
Where have you hid the quiver of oratory
until today, dear child, that now you dare
to go and see the Sovereign on such business?
A sudden ray of hope refreshes me!

NATALIA

God will give arrows that will hit the mark.
But if the Elector cannot, cannot change
the sentence of the law, you will, I trust,
a brave man, bravely acquiesce in it.
A victor during life a thousand times
can be victorious also in his death.

THE ELECTRESS

Away! The favorable moment passes.

THE PRINCE OF HOMBURG

May all the saints protect you! Now, farewell!
Farewell! No matter what you may achieve,
let me receive a sign of your success!

(*exeunt*)

ACT FOUR

SCENE ONE

Chamber of the ELECTOR.
The ELECTOR *stands at a table, holding some papers. There are lights on the table.* PRINCESS NATALIA *enters through the center door and kneels at some distance from the* ELECTOR. *Pause.*

PRINCESS NATALIA (*kneeling*)
My noble uncle, Frederick of the March!

THE ELECTOR (*putting the papers aside*)
Natalia!
(*He tries to raise her.*)

NATALIA
                    Please!

THE ELECTOR
                                        What do you wish, my dear?

NATALIA
Before your feet, as it befits my station,
to plead with you to pardon cousin Homburg.
I do not want him rescued for myself —
My heart desires him and confesses it —
I do not want him rescued for myself;
let him take any wife that he may wish.
I merely want him in existence, uncle,
apart, free, independent, on his own,

71

just like a flower in which I take delight.
This I entreat of you, my lord and friend,
and know you will give ear to such entreaty.

THE ELECTOR (*raising her*)

What are you saying there, my little daughter?
You know of cousin Homburg's recent crime?

NATALIA

Dear uncle!

THE ELECTOR

                    Tell me: Was it not a crime?

NATALIA

This blue-eyed, blond offender, my dear uncle,
whom, still before he stammers his entreaty,
forgiveness should be raising from the ground —
you surely will not kick him from your side!
If only for his mother's sake, who bore him,
you will embrace him, saying: "Do not weep!
I value you as loyalty itself."
Was it not ardor for your name and glory
which lured him at the moment of the battle
to break the barrier of the law? And then,
the barrier broken after youthful fashion,
did he not crush the dragon like a man?
To crown him first as victor, then behead him
is not what history calls on you to do.
That would be so dispassionate, dearest uncle,
that one might almost label it inhuman.
And God has never made a milder man!

THE ELECTOR

My darling child! Look: If I were a tyrant
your speech, I feel it keenly, would have melted

my heart already in my granite breast.
Give me your own advice: May I suppress
the sentence which the judges have pronounced?
What do you think would be the consequence?

NATALIA

For whom? For you?

THE ELECTOR

                    For me? No. — What? For me?
Do you know nothing higher, maid, than me?
Are you quite ignorant about a shrine
that in the camp is known as fatherland?

NATALIA

Why this concern, Sire? Will this fatherland
at once be shattered and go down in ruin
because you're moved to mercy in this case?
Rather, what you, who have been reared in camp,
call lack of order — arbitrarily
to annul the judges' sentence in this case —
appears to me to be the height of order.
The laws of war, I know full well, shall govern,
but so shall tenderhearted sentiments.
The fatherland that you have founded for us
stands like a solid fortress, noble uncle;
it's bound to weather still quite different storms
than this unsanctioned victory. In the future
it will develop splendidly, expand
at grandchild's hands, become more beautiful,
with pinnacles, abundant, fairylike,
a joy to friends, a terror to all foes.
It does not need this cold and dreary bond
of friendly blood in order to survive

the peaceful grandeur of my uncle's autumn.

THE ELECTOR

Does cousin Homburg think so?

NATALIA

Cousin Homburg?

THE ELECTOR

He thinks it does not matter to his country
if impulse governs in it or the law?

NATALIA

Oh, this young man!

THE ELECTOR

Well, does he?

NATALIA

Oh, dear uncle!

To that my only answer is to weep.

THE ELECTOR (*taken aback*)

Why so, my little daughter? What has happened?

NATALIA (*hesitant*)

He thinks of only one thing: to be rescued.
The soldiers' barrels, raised to shoulder height,
revolt him so that, shocked and in confusion,
he has but one desire: to stay alive.
He could look on as all of Brandenburg
is swallowed up, with thunderclaps and lightning,
and would not even ask, "What's happening?"
Oh, what a hero's heart you've broken!
(*She turns away, crying.*)

THE ELECTOR (*utterly amazed*)

No,

dearest Natalia, no! Impossible!
You say he's begging mercy?

NATALIA

Oh, if only
you never, never had condemned him!

THE ELECTOR

No,
tell me: He's begging mercy? God in heaven!
What's happened, my dear child? Why are you crying?
You've seen him? Tell me everything! You've seen him?

NATALIA (*leaning against his breast*)

This very moment, up in Aunt's apartment,
where in the dusk with coat and hat he slipped,
perturbed and shy, in secret, quite unworthy,
a lamentable and unpleasant sight.
Nobody praised by history as its hero
could fall into such misery I had thought.
Look: I'm a woman and recoil in fright
at any worm that may approach my heel;
however, death in horrid lion's shape
would not find me so crushed, so disconcerted,
so utterly devoid of heroism. —
Oh, what is human greatness, human glory!

THE ELECTOR (*confused*)

Well, then, by God of heaven and of earth,
take courage, child! He's free.

NATALIA

My Lord?

THE ELECTOR

He's pardoned.
I'll send the appropriate note to him at once.

NATALIA

O dearest! Is it really true?

THE ELECTOR

You've heard!

NATALIA

He shall be pardoned? Now he will not die?

THE ELECTOR

Upon my oath! I swear it. How could I
oppose the view of such a man-at-war?
His intuition, as you're well aware,
deep in my heart I hold in great respect.
If he can think the sentence is unjust,
the articles are set aside; he's free.
(*He brings her a chair.*)
Will you sit down a moment?
(*He goes to the table, sits down, and writes. Pause*)

NATALIA (*aside*)

O my heart,
why are you knocking at your house this way?

THE ELECTOR (*writing*)

The Prince is in the castle still?

NATALIA

Your pardon!
He has gone back to his imprisonment.

THE ELECTOR (*finishes and seals his letter and takes it to
NATALIA*)

My little niece, my little daughter cried!
And I, to whom her pleasure is entrusted,
clouded the sky of her delightful eyes!
(*He puts his arm around her waist.*)
You want to take the note to him yourself?

NATALIA

Into the prison, you mean?

THE ELECTOR (*giving her the letter*)

                      Why not? — Ho, haiduks!

(*enter* HAIDUKS)

The coach is wanted at the gate. The Princess
has business with Commander Homburg.

(HAIDUKS *exeunt*)

                          Well:

He'll have a chance to thank you for his life.

(*He embraces her.*)

Now you're no longer angry with me, child?

NATALIA (*after a pause*)

What caused your favor, Sire, so suddenly
I do not know and will not scrutinize.
However, this I'm sure of in my heart:
You would not be unkind and scoff at me.
No matter what this letter may contain,
I do believe his rescue — and I thank you.

(*She kisses his hand.*)

THE ELECTOR

Why certainly, my daughter, certainly!
As sure as cousin Homburg wishes it.

(*exeunt*)

SCENE TWO

Chamber of PRINCESS NATALIA. *Enter* PRINCESS NATALIA,
followed by two LADIES-IN-WAITING *and* COUNT REUSS.

PRINCESS NATALIA (*in a hurry*)

What do you bring, Count? — From the regiment?
Is it important? Can it wait a day?

COUNT REUSS (*giving her a letter*)

    An envelope from Colonel Kottwitz, Madam!

NATALIA

    Quick! Let me have it! What is in it, Count?
    (*She opens the envelope.*)

REUSS

    A candid but respectful supplication
    in favor of our commander, Prince of Homburg,
    directed to the Sovereign.

NATALIA (*reading*)

                  "Supplication
    humbly submitted by the Regiment
    Princess of Orange."
    (*pause*)

              Who's the author, Count?

REUSS

    Kottwitz himself; his awkward hand betrays him.
    Besides, his noble name is listed first.

NATALIA

    And, then — the thirty other signatures?

REUSS

    The staff of officers, by rank, my lady.

NATALIA

    And now this supplication comes to me?

REUSS

    Yes, Princess, with the humble inquiry
    if you, as chief, will place your name atop.
    (*pause*)

NATALIA

    In fact, I hear the Sovereign on his own

intends to pardon my distinguished cousin,
and such a step will not be necessary.

REUSS (*pleased*)

Really?

NATALIA

Still, wisely used, this sheet may influence him;
it might be welcome, too, as cause for action.
Thus, I will not refuse my signature
and, following your request, I place my name
atop of yours.
(*She is about to write.*)

REUSS

You'll earn our fervent thanks.
(*pause*)

NATALIA (*again turning to him*)

I see my regiment only, Count of Reuss.
Why do I miss the Bomsdorf cuirassiers,
The Gött dragoons, and those of Anhalt-Pless?

REUSS

Not, as perhaps you fear, because their hearts
beat for him not as warmly as do ours.
Unfortunately Kottwitz is in Arnstein,
divided from those other regiments,
which have been stationed here around this town.
The paper cannot with facility
unfold its strength in all directions.

NATALIA

Yet,
this way, I think, it does not carry weight?
Count, are you certain, if you were in town

and saw the gentlemen assembled here,
they also would accede to this petition?

REUSS

Here in the town, my Lady? In a body!
All of the cavalry would commit itself
by signature. In fact, the chances are
that such subscription could successfully
extend to all the troops of Brandenburg.

NATALIA (*after a pause*)

Why not dispatch some of your officers
to look into the business here in town?

REUSS

Your pardon! That the colonel would not do:
he would not, he declared, take any action
that could be baptized with an evil name.

NATALIA

Strange gentleman! Now bold, now diffident!
By chance the Elector, pressed by other business —
I now remember — issued me instructions
to order Kottwitz here, the reason being
that stabling is too cramped in his encampment.
I'll sit down right away to attend to it.
(*She sits down and writes.*)

REUSS

By heaven, excellent, Princess! No event
could favor more the cause of this petition.

NATALIA (*writing*)

Use it as best you can, dear Count of Reuss!
(*She finishes, seals the envelope, and rises.*)
Meanwhile, please understand, this note remains
within your wallet: you will not depart

for Arnstein with it and report to Kottwitz
until I give you more precise instructions.
(*She gives him the note.*)

A HAIDUK (*entering*)

The carriage, Princess, by the Sovereign's orders,
stands ready in the yard, awaiting you.

NATALIA

Then bring it to the gate! I'm coming down.
(*Pause. Pensive,* NATALIA *steps to the table and puts on
her gloves.*)
I want to see the Prince of Homburg, Count.
Perhaps you'd like to keep me company?
A place is open for you in my carriage.

REUSS

My Princess, what an honor!
(*He offers her his arm.*)

NATALIA (*to the* LADIES-IN-WAITING)

                              Come with me! —
I may decide about the letter there.
(*exeunt*)

SCENE THREE

The PRINCE OF HOMBURG'S *prison.*
The PRINCE OF HOMBURG *hangs his hat on the wall and
slumps down on a cushion on the floor.*

THE PRINCE OF HOMBURG

Life is a journey, say the dervishes,
and quite a short one. Yes, of course: two spans

above the ground to two spans under it. —
I want to sit down at the halfway mark. —
Who wears his head today still on his shoulders
hangs it tomorrow, trembling, on his body;
another day, and by his heel it lies. —
They say a sun shines in those parts as well,
and over even gayer fields than here.
No doubt. A pity that the eyes are rotting
which are to see all that magnificence!

SCENE FOUR

Enter PRINCESS NATALIA *on* COUNT REUSS' *arm, preceded by a* RUNNER *with a torch and followed by* LADIES-IN-WAIT- ING. *The* PRINCE OF HOMBURG

THE RUNNER

Her Highness Princess Orange is approaching.

THE PRINCE OF HOMBURG (*rising*)

Natalia!

THE RUNNER

Here she is herself.

PRINCESS NATALIA (*bowing to* COUNT REUSS)

Count Reuss,

leave us alone a moment!

(REUSS *and the* RUNNER *exeunt.*)

THE PRINCE OF HOMBURG

My dear Princess!

NATALIA

Dear cousin!

THE PRINCE OF HOMBURG (*leading her to the foreground*)
                    Tell me! Speak! What do you bring?

NATALIA

Good news! All's well. Just as I had predicted,
you have been pardoned, set at liberty.
This letter, by his hand, corroborates it.

THE PRINCE OF HOMBURG

No! It's impossible! I must be dreaming!

NATALIA

Read! Read the letter! You will find it so.

THE PRINCE OF HOMBURG (*reading*)

"My Prince of Homburg: When I had you put in prison
because of your precipitate attack,
it seemed to me I only did my duty.
I counted on your own approval then.
If you believe you've suffered an injustice,
please tell me briefly, and at once
I will return your saber."

(NATALIA *pales. Pause. The* PRINCE *looks at her questioningly*.)

NATALIA (*with an expression of sudden joy*)
                    There, you see!
You merely have to let him know in brief — !
My dear, beloved friend!
(*She presses his hand.*)

THE PRINCE OF HOMBURG

                    My dearest Princess!

NATALIA

Oh blessed hour that now unfolds itself!
Here, take it! Here's the pen. Take it and write!

THE PRINCE OF HOMBURG

And here the signature?

NATALIA

The F; his mark. —
Miss Bork! Aren't you delighted? — Oh, his mildness
is limitless — I knew it — like the sea.
Come, bring a chair! He shall reply at once.

THE PRINCE OF HOMBURG

He says: If I believe — ?

NATALIA (*interrupting*)

Of course! Now, quick!
Sit down! I'll dictate your reply to him.
(*She offers him a chair.*)

THE PRINCE OF HOMBURG

I want to read the letter once again.

NATALIA (*snatching the letter from his hand*)

With what in mind? Have you not seen your tomb
gape at you near the church with open jaws?
You have no time to waste. Sit down and write!

THE PRINCE OF HOMBURG (*smiling*)

In truth, you're acting now as if the grave
were set to pounce upon me like a panther.
(*He sits down and takes a pen.*)

NATALIA (*turning away in tears*)

Write if you do not want to make me angry!
(*The* PRINCE *rings for a servant. A* SERVANT *enters.*)

THE PRINCE OF HOMBURG

Bring paper and a pen, and wax and seal!
(*The* SERVANT *fetches them and leaves. The* PRINCE
writes. Pause)

THE PRINCE OF HOMBURG (*tearing up the beginning of a letter and throwing it under the table*)

A stupid start!

(*He takes another sheet.*)

NATALIA (*after picking up the letter*)

Your pardon? What was that?

Why, this is good; this is exceptional!

THE PRINCE OF HOMBURG (*muttering*)

Pooh! It's a scoundrel's, not a prince's wording.

I'll have to put it in another way.

(*Pause. He holds out his hand for the* ELECTOR's *letter, which* NATALIA *is holding.*)

Exactly what is stated in his letter?

NATALIA (*refusing it*)

Nothing at all.

THE PRINCE OF HOMBURG

Please!

NATALIA

You have read it.

THE PRINCE OF HOMBURG (*catching hold of it*)

Still!

I want to know how to express myself.

(*He unfolds the letter and reads it over.*)

NATALIA (*aside*)

O God in heaven! Now he's done for.

THE PRINCE OF HOMBURG (*taken aback*)

Look!

Well! Very strange indeed! Upon my life!

You've overlooked this passage?

NATALIA

No. — Which one?

THE PRINCE OF HOMBURG

He asks that I myself decide the matter.

NATALIA

Well?

THE PRINCE OF HOMBURG

Very honest; very dignified!
The very words of noble-mindedness!

NATALIA

My friend, his generosity is boundless.
But now do your part, too, and write to him
as he desires. You see what's needed now
is just a pretext, just an outward form:
once he receives the note, immediately
the whole affair is over.

THE PRINCE OF HOMBURG (*putting the letter aside*)

No, my dear.
I want to think it over till tomorrow.

NATALIA

Inexplicable man! What turn is this?
Why? For what purpose?

THE PRINCE OF HOMBURG (*rising from his chair, emphatically*)

Do not ask me, please!
You have not weighed the contents of the letter.
I cannot write him in the circumstances
that he has done me wrong. If in this mood
you force me to deliver him an answer,
by God, I'll tell him, "You have done me right!"
(*He sits down at the table again, arms folded, and re-reads the letter.*)

NATALIA (*pale*)

You're mad! What are you saying?
(*Moved, she bends over him.*)

THE PRINCE OF HOMBURG (*pressing her hand*)

Just one moment!

It seems to me —
(*He meditates.*)

NATALIA

I beg your pardon?

THE PRINCE OF HOMBURG

Wait!

The appropriate words will come to me at once.

NATALIA (*pained*)

Homburg!

THE PRINCE OF HOMBURG (*taking the pen*)

What is it?

NATALIA

My beloved friend!
I praise your impulse, but I warrant you:
The regiment is ready which, appeased,
shall hold your obsequies with carbine salvos
over the hillock of your grave tomorrow.
If, noble as you are, you can't resist
the sentence, cannot act to cancel it,
as he requests it from you in this letter,
well, I assure you, as the matter stands,
he will adopt a lofty attitude
and, full of pity, have you executed.

THE PRINCE OF HOMBURG (*writing*)

All right.

NATALIA

All right?

THE PRINCE OF HOMBURG

Let him act as he may;
in turn, I must proceed here as I should.

NATALIA (*frightened, stepping closer*)

Fantastic man, you are not really writing —

THE PRINCE OF HOMBURG (*finishing*)

"Signed, Homburg, Fehrbellin, the twelfth." — I've finished.

Frank!

(*He puts the letter in an envelope and seals the envelope.*)

NATALIA

O my God in heaven!

THE PRINCE OF HOMBURG (*rising, to the* SERVANT *who has
entered*)

Take this letter!
Deliver it to the Sovereign at the castle!
(*Exit the* SERVANT.)
He faces me with dignity, and I
will not confront him an unworthy man.
Important guilt, I know, weighs on my chest.
If I must argue with him for my pardon,
I do not want to hear about his mercy.

NATALIA (*kissing him*)

Receive this kiss! Now, if a dozen bullets
pierced you aground, I could not hold myself:
I'd jubilate and weep and say: I like you. —
Meanwhile, if you do what your heart demands,

I should be free to follow mine. — Count Reuss!
(*The door is opened by a* RUNNER. REUSS *enters.*)

REUSS

Here!

NATALIA

Off with you to Arnstein now!
Present your letter there to Colonel Kottwitz!
The Sovereign wants the regiment to march.
I shall expect it here in town by midnight.
(*exeunt*)

ACT FIVE

SCENE ONE

Hall in the castle.
Enter the ELECTOR, *half dressed, from the adjoining chamber. He is followed by* COUNT TRUCHSS, COUNT HOHENZOLLERN, *and* CAPTAIN GOLZ. — PAGES *with lights.*

THE ELECTOR

Kottwitz? The Princess' regiment? In town?

COUNT TRUCHSS (*opening the window*)

Yes, Sire. He stands deployed before the castle.

THE ELECTOR

Well? Solve this puzzle for me, gentlemen!
Who called him here?

COUNT HOHENZOLLERN

I do not know, my Sovereign.

THE ELECTOR

I have assigned him Arnstein as his station.—
Let someone hurry down and bring him here!

CAPTAIN GOLZ

He'll presently appear before you, Sire.

THE ELECTOR

Where is he?

GOLZ

> In the Council Hall, I hear,
> where all the commandants that serve your house
> are gathered.

THE ELECTOR

> For what purpose?

HOHENZOLLERN

> I don't know.

TRUCHSS

> Permit, my Lord and Sovereign, that we, too,
> repair there for a moment!

THE ELECTOR

> Where, you say?
> The Council Hall?

HOHENZOLLERN

> To join the gathering there.
> We gave our word to put in an appearance.

THE ELECTOR (*after a brief pause*)

> You are dismissed.

GOLZ

> Come, my dear gentlemen!

(*Exeunt the* OFFICERS.)

SCENE TWO

The ELECTOR. — *Later two* SERVANTS.

THE ELECTOR

> How strange! — Were I the Dey of Tunis, now
> I'd sound the alarm in such ambiguous case.

I'd put the silken cord upon my table,
and at the gate, all blocked with palisades,
I'd have them draw up howitzers and cannon.
But as it is Hans Kottwitz from the Priegnitz
who's coming here highhanded, on his own,
I will proceed as it befits the march.
Three silver locks there are atop his skull;
I take one; then, with his twelve squadrons, gently
I lead him back to Arnstein, to his station.
Why should the town be wakened from its sleep?
(*After again stepping to the window for a moment, he
goes to the table and rings a bell. Two* SERVANTS *enter.*)

THE ELECTOR

Rush down and ask, as in your own behalf,
What's happening at the Council Hall!

FIRST SERVANT

                                        Yes, Sire!

(*exit*)

THE ELECTOR (*to the other* SERVANT)

And you, you go and bring my clothes to me!
(*The* SERVANT *goes and brings the* ELECTOR'S *clothes.
The* ELECTOR *dresses and puts on his regalia.*)

SCENE THREE

Enter MARSHAL DÖRFLING. *The others.*

MARSHAL DÖRFLING

Rebellion, Sire!

THE ELECTOR (*still dressing*)
      Be still, be still!
To come into my chamber unannounced
is hateful to me, as you're well aware.
What do you want?

THE MARSHAL
      Sire, an event — forgive me —
of special moment leads me here to you.
Without instructions, Colonel Kottwitz moved
here into town; some hundred officers
are gathered round him in the Hall of Knights.
A sheet is circulating in their ranks
intended to encroach upon your rights.

THE ELECTOR
I am aware of it. What can it be
except a motion in the Prince's favor,
who has been sentenced to the firing squad?

THE MARSHAL
Quite so. By God, you've hit it on the head.

THE ELECTOR
All right. My heart is in their midst.

THE MARSHAL
         I hear
the madmen plan to come to see you here
and hand you their petition presently.
Then, if unreconciled you should insist
upon the sentence — dare I tell you this? —
they intend by force to free him from his prison.

THE ELECTOR (*somberly*)
Who's told you that?

THE MARSHAL

                    Who's told me? Lady Retzow,
whom you can trust, a cousin of my wife's.
She was at Bailiff Retzow's house, her uncle's,
and there some officers who'd come from camp
spoke loudly of this daring enterprise.

THE ELECTOR

A man must tell me that ere I believe it.
Why, with my boot set down before his house
from these young heroes I defend him!

THE MARSHAL

                                        Sire,
let me beseech you: If it is at all
your will to grant a pardon to the Prince,
do so before an odious step is taken!
You know how every army loves its hero:
do not allow this spark that glows in it
to spread at will as a devouring fire!
Kottwitz and those he's gathered here as yet
don't know that I've forewarned you loyally;
before he comes, return the Prince his sword,
return it, as he after all deserves!
You'll give the journal one more noble deed
and one less awful deed to write about.

THE ELECTOR

First I would have to ask the Prince's view,
for arbitrariness, as you must know,
did not imprison him nor can free him now. —
I'll see the gentlemen when they arrive.

THE MARSHAL (aside)

Confound it! He's prepared against all arrows.

SCENE FOUR

Enter two HAIDUKS, *one holding an envelope. The others.*

FIRST HAIDUK

Sire, Colonel Kottwitz, Hennings, Truchss, and others request an audience.

THE ELECTOR (*to the other* HAIDUK, *taking the envelope from him*)

From the Prince of Homburg?

SECOND HAIDUK

Yes, Highness!

THE ELECTOR

And who gave the letter to you?

SECOND HAIDUK

The Swiss who's standing watch down at the gate;
he got it from the Prince's orderly.

THE ELECTOR (*steps to the table and reads, then turns and calls to a* PAGE)

Go bring the sentence to me, Prittwitz. — Furthermore, I want Count Horn's, the Swedish envoy's, passport.
(*Exit the* PAGE.)
(*to the first* HAIDUK)
Have Kottwitz and his company come in!

SCENE FIVE

Enter COLONEL KOTTWITZ *and* COLONEL HENNINGS, COUNT TRUCHSS, COUNT HOHENZOLLERN *and* COUNT SPARREN, COUNT REUSS, CAPTAIN GOLZ *and* CAPTAIN STRANZ, *and other* OFFICERS. *The others.*

COLONEL KOTTWITZ (*with the petition*)

Allow me, on behalf of all our army,

humbly to hand you this, august Elector!

THE ELECTOR

Kottwitz, before I take this paper, tell me:

By whom have you been summoned to this town?

KOTTWITZ (*looking at him*)

With the dragoons?

THE ELECTOR

　　　　　　　Yes, with the regiment.

I had assigned you Arnstein as your station.

KOTTWITZ

Your order, Sire, has called me to this place.

THE ELECTOR

Indeed? Show me that order!

KOTTWITZ

　　　　　　　Here, my Sovereign.

THE ELECTOR (*reading*)

"Given, Natalia, Fehrbellin, by order

of Frederick, my most estimable uncle."

KOTTWITZ

By God, my Lord and Sovereign, I do hope

this order is not unknown to you.

THE ELECTOR

　　　　　　　No, no,

you see — What person handed you this order?

KOTTWITZ

Count Reuss.

THE ELECTOR (*after a moment's pause*)

　　　　　　Indeed I'd like to welcome you.

To General Homburg, who received his sentence,

you and your dozen squadrons are appointed
to pay the final honors in the morning.

KOTTWITZ (*taken aback*)

I beg your pardon, Sire?

THE ELECTOR (*returning the order to him*)
                      The regiment
is at the gate still at this time of night?

KOTTWITZ

The night, you see —

THE ELECTOR

                        Why has it not moved in?

KOTTWITZ

It has moved in, my Sovereign. By your order,
it has been quartered in this town.

THE ELECTOR (*turning toward the window*)
                        Indeed?
A while ago — ? By heaven, in that case
you found your stabling quickly. All the better!
I bid you welcome once again. — Now say:
What is the news you have? What brings you here?

KOTTWITZ

This plea, Sire, by your loyal troops.

THE ELECTOR

                        Let's see it!

KOTTWITZ

The word, however, which escaped your lips
is dashing all my hopes.

THE ELECTOR

                    Another word
again can raise them.

(*He reads.*)

      .   "Supplication, begging
a sovereign pardon for our indicted chief,
the General Frederick, Prince of Hesse-Homburg."
(*to the officers*)
A noble name, my lords; it well deserves
your standing up for it in such array.
(*He looks at the paper again.*)
Who drafted this petition?

KOTTWITZ

                I did, Sire.

THE ELECTOR

The Prince has been informed about the contents?

KOTTWITZ

Not in the slightest way. Among ourselves
was it conceived and finished.

THE ELECTOR

                Let me see!
(*He steps to the table and looks through the paper.
Long pause*)
Hm! This is curious. Veteran though you are,
you shield the Prince's action, justify
his unsolicited attack on Wrangel?

KOTTWITZ

Yes, Sire; that is what Kottwitz does.

THE ELECTOR

                      However,
you did not think so on the battlefield.

KOTTWITZ

I had not weighed it properly, my Sovereign.
I should have calmly yielded to the Prince,

for he's an expert in the art of war.
The left wing of the Swedes was giving way,
the right wing was engaged in reinforcement;
if he had stayed, awaiting your command,
they would have gained new footholds in the gorges,
and you would not have scored your victory, Sire.

THE ELECTOR

I see. You please to assume that! As you know,
I sent off Colonel Hennings to remove
the Swedish bridgehead guarding Wrangel's rear.
If you had not infringed upon my orders,
this stroke by Hennings would have been successful;
within two hours he would have burned the bridges
and taken up positions on the Rhyn,
and Wrangel in the ditches and the marsh
would have been brought to ruin, root and branch.

KOTTWITZ

It is the bunglers' business, Sire, not yours,
to want to gain the highest crown of fate.
So far you've always taken what it offered.
The froward dragon that despoiled your march
was forced to run away with bloody brain.
What more could happen in a single day?
What does it matter if another fortnight
he mends his wounds, exhausted, in the sand?
We've learned the art of beating him in combat
and are intent on practicing it further.
Let us meet Wrangel, man to man, again
with all our vigor! That will be the finish,
and he will fly into the Baltic Sea.
Rome was not put together in a day.

THE ELECTOR

You fool, how can you hope for that to happen
if on the battle chariot anyone
may seize my reins, according to his will?
You think that fortune always, as this time,
will grant a wreath for insubordination?
I want no victory which accrues to me
a child of chance. My wish is to maintain
legality, the mother of my dominion,
that bears whole families of victories for me.

KOTTWITZ

The highest, the supreme legality
which is to govern in your generals' hearts —
that, Sire, is not the letter of your will;
it is the fatherland, it is the crown,
it is yourself, upon whose head it rests.
What do you really care about the rule
by which your enemy is defeated if
he drops with all his banners at your feet?
The rule that beats him — that one is the highest.
Our army, clinging ardently to you —
is it to be a tool, alike your sword,
which lifeless stays within your golden belt?
The miserable, unprophetic spirit
that first proclaimed this precept, and the poor,
shortsighted statesmanship which, for one case
where sentiment proves ruinous, quite forgets
ten other cases, in the circumstances,
where sentiment alone can bring salvation!
I do not shed my blood for you in battle
for payment — be it money or renown.

May God forbid! It is too good for that.
In quiet, by myself, free, independent,
I take delight in your magnificence,
the splendor and the growth of your great name.
That is the wage for which my heart is sold.
Grant that for this unbidden victory now
you doom the Prince to die, and I tomorrow,
together with my squadrons, like a shepherd,
encounter victory, unsolicited,
amid the forests and the rocks somewhere:
by God, I'd really have to be a scoundrel
not blithely to repeat the Prince's action.
And if, the code of law in hand, you said,
"Kottwitz, you've forfeited your head," I'd say:
"I knew that, Sire. Here, take it! It is yours.
When with an oath I fastened to your crown
with heart and soul, I did not bar my head.
I'd give you nothing that is not your own."

THE ELECTOR

You, strange old man, are more than I can handle.
Your speech bribes me with cunning oratory —
me, who you know am fond of you. Therefore,
I'll call an advocate to put an end to this;
he will conduct my case.
(*He rings. Enter a* SERVANT.)

                              The Prince of Homburg —
let him be brought here from his prison!
(*Exit the* SERVANT.)

                                        He will,
I warrant you, instruct you in the meaning
of discipline of warfare and obedience.

At least, a note he sent me is at odds
with your sophistic principle of freedom,
which you expounded to me like a child.
(*He steps to the table again and reads.*)

KOTTWITZ (*amazed*)

Bring whom? Call whom?

COLONEL HENNINGS

The Prince?

COUNT TRUCHSS

Impossible!

(*The* OFFICERS, *disturbed, talk among themselves.*)

THE ELECTOR

And who's the author of this second letter?

COUNT HOHENZOLLERN

I am, Sire.

THE ELECTOR (*reading*)

"Proof that Frederick, the Elector,
the Prince's deed himself" — By heaven!
I call that bold!
What? You're accusing me of having caused the crime
that he committed in the course of battle?

HOHENZOLLERN

Yes, you, my Elector; I am, Hohenzollern!

THE ELECTOR

Well then, by God; that passes even fiction.
one man explains to me he bears no guilt,
the other man that I'm the guilty one! —
How do you mean to prove this thesis to me?

HOHENZOLLERN

You will recall the night, Sire, in the garden,
when under planes we found the Prince asleep.

He might have dreamed of victory on the morrow,
for in his hands he held some laurel leaves.
As if to probe into his inmost soul,
you took his wreath and, smiling, wound around it
the golden chain you wear about your neck.
Thus joined, you gave the garland and the chain
to young Natalia, your distinguished niece.
The Prince turns crimson at such wondrous sight.
He rises to obtain these lovely things,
held out to him by such beloved hands.
But you, retreating quickly with the Princess,
withdraw from him; the gate receives you; vanished
are maiden, chain, and wreath of laurel leaves.
And solitary, holding in his hand
a glove he snatched — he does not know from whom —
he stays behind, enveloped by the night.

THE ELECTOR

What glove was that?

HOHENZOLLERN

                    Please let me finish, Sire!
The whole thing was a jest; but how important
it was to him I realized at once.
For when, as if by chance, I sneak to him,
approaching through the back door of the garden,
and waken him and he collects his senses,
the memory overwhelms him with delight.
You can't imagine anything more touching.
The whole event, as if it were a dream,
at once he tells me to the smallest detail.
So vividly, he thinks, he'd never dreamed.
He forms the firm conviction that the heavens

have augured him that all his mind has seen —
the maiden, laurel wreath, and ornament —
God will award him on the day of battle.

THE ELECTOR

Hm! Strange! And what about the glove?

HOHENZOLLERN

                                    Well, Sire —

that fragment of the dream, incorporated,
destroys as well as strengthens his conviction.
At first he looks at it with widened eyes —
the color is white, it seems by type and shape
to be a lady's. On that evening, though,
he did not meet with any in the garden
who might have lost it. Then I cross his fancies
and call him to the castle for the briefing.
So he forgets what is beyond his grasp
and, absentminded, puts the glove away.

THE ELECTOR

And then?

HOHENZOLLERN

                    Then, with his tablet and his pencil,
he goes inside to hear the battle orders
with rapt attention from the Marshal's mouth.
The Electress and the Princess, it so happens,
prepared to leave, are also in the hall.
Who can imagine his immense amazement
when now the Princess finds she's lost the glove
he's carrying in his pocket? Several times
the Marshal calls him. "What's my Marshal's pleasure?"
he answers, trying to collect his thoughts;
but, what with wonders on his every side —

a thunderbolt from heaven could have struck —
(*He pauses.*)

THE ELECTOR

Was it the Princess' glove?

HOHENZOLLERN

It was indeed.
(*The* ELECTOR *is lost in thought.*)

HOHENZOLLERN (*continuing*)

He's like a stone; the pencil in his hand,
he's standing there apparently alive,
but his sensation, as by magic blows,
is gone, and not until the following morning,
while cannon fire is thundering in the ranks,
does he return to life again and asks:
"Dear Henry, tell me what it was last night
that Dörfling had to say concerning me!"

MARSHAL DÖRFLING

Sire, truly I subscribe to this account.
The Prince, I recollect, did not perceive
a word of what I said. I'd seen him often
withdrawn in thought, but not to such extent,
with heart and soul, as on that certain day.

THE ELECTOR

And now, if I correctly understand you,
you're building me this sort of syllogism:
Had I not jested in ambiguous fashion
with this young dreamer, there would be no guilt;
he would not have been dreamy at the briefing
or stubborn in the battle. Is that so?
Is that so? Is that your opinion?

HOHENZOLLERN

                 Sire,
to draw the inference now is up to you.

THE ELECTOR

Oh, what a feebleminded fool you are!
Had you not called me down into the garden,
I would not, prompted by curiosity,
innocuously have jested with this dreamer.
Thus, I maintain with fully equal right
that it was you who brought about his blunder. —
The Delphic wisdom of my officers!

HOHENZOLLERN

It is enough, my Elector. I'm convinced
my words fell like a weight into your heart.

SCENE SIX

Enter an OFFICER. *The others.*

THE OFFICER

The Prince, Sire, will appear in just a moment.

THE ELECTOR

All right, then. Let him enter!

THE OFFICER

                   In two minutes.
He had the churchyard opened on the way.

THE ELECTOR

The churchyard?

THE OFFICER

            Yes, my Lord and Sovereign.

THE ELECTOR

Why?

THE OFFICER

To tell the truth, I do not know. However,
it seemed he wanted to behold the tomb
that your command had opened for him there.
(*The* COMMANDERS *gather to speak to each other.*)

THE ELECTOR

No matter. Have him enter when he comes!
(*He steps to the table again and looks into the papers.*)

COUNT TRUCHSS

I see the guard approaching with the Prince.

SCENE SEVEN

Enter THE PRINCE OF HOMBURG. *An* OFFICER *with a* GUARD.
The others.

THE ELECTOR

I'm asking your assistance, my young Prince.
Look: Colonel Kottwitz, here in your behalf,
has brought this paper with the signatures
of scores of noblemen, in long succession.
They say the military wants you freed
and disapproves the sentence of the court.
Read, if you please, and find out for yourself!
(*He hands the paper to him.*)

THE PRINCE OF HOMBURG (*glances at the paper; then, looking around among the* OFFICERS)

My old friend, Kottwitz, let me grasp your hand!

You're doing more for me than I deserved
the day of battle. Hurry back again
to Arnstein presently, from where you came,
and do not stir, for I've made up my mind:
I want to die the death decreed for me.
(*He hands the paper to him.*)

COLONEL KOTTWITZ (*taken aback*)

No, by no means, my Prince! What are you saying?

COUNT HOHENZOLLERN

He wants the death —

COUNT TRUCHSS

He shall and must not die!

SEVERAL OFFICERS (*surging forward*)

My Sovereign and Elector! Hear us, Sire!

THE PRINCE OF HOMBURG

Silence! It is my inflexible desire.
I want to glorify the sacred law
of war, which I infringed before our army,
by dying freely. Of what value, brothers,
can one more meager victory be to you
which I perhaps still wrest away from Wrangel
compared with glorious triumph on the morrow
over the most destructive adversary
within us — obstinacy, recklessness?
The stranger shall succumb who would subdue us,
and free shall stay the people of Brandenburg
on their maternal soil, their own possession,
with all the splendid fields created for them!

KOTTWITZ (*moved*)

My son, my dearest friend — what shall I call you?

TRUCHSS

O God in heaven!

KOTTWITZ

Let me kiss your hand!

(*They gather around him.*)

THE PRINCE OF HOMBURG (*turning to the* ELECTOR)

My Sovereign, you who bore a sweeter name
for me once — now unfortunately lost —
I lay myself impassioned at your feet.
Forgive if on the fateful day I served you
with overhasty eagerness: my death
now purges me of any guilt I bear.
Console my heart, which, reconciled, serenely
surrenders to your sentence: let it know
that your breast, too, renounces any grudge,
and as a token in this hour of leave
grant me a favor graciously!

THE ELECTOR

Speak up,
my brave young man! What is it you desire?
I pledge my word to you and knightly honor:
No matter what it is, I grant it to you.

THE PRINCE OF HOMBURG

Sire, do not purchase with your niece's hand
the peace from Gustaf Karl! Send from the camp
the envoy of this infamous proposal,
and let a rain of bullets be his answer!

THE ELECTOR (*kissing his forehead*)

It shall be as you say. Now, with this kiss
I grant this last request of yours, my son.
Besides, what need is there of that concession,

wrung from me only by the war's misfortune?
For now from every single word of yours
grows me a victory that suppresses him.
She's Prince of Homburg's bride, I'll write to him —
who was condemned because of Fehrbellin —
and he should try to wrest her from his spirit,
which leads the banners on the battlefield.
(*He kisses him once more and raises him.*)

THE PRINCE OF HOMBURG

Now, Sire, you've given me my life. Now I
implore for you all blessing from above
which from their throne of clouds the seraphim
pour, jubilating, down on heroes' heads.
Go and wage war, Sire, overcome the world
that dares stand up to you, for you deserve it!

THE ELECTOR

Guard, go and lead the Prince back to his prison!

SCENE EIGHT

PRINCESS NATALIA *and the* ELECTRESS *appear in the door.*
Follow LADIES-IN-WAITING. *The others.*

PRINCESS NATALIA

Please, mother! Why speak of propriety?
To love him is the highest in such hour! —
My cherished, miserable friend!

THE PRINCE OF HOMBURG (*leaving*)

Away!

COUNT TRUCHSS (*holding him back*)

   No, by no means, my Prince!

   (*Several* OFFICERS *bar the* PRINCE'S *way.*)

THE PRINCE OF HOMBURG

                    Lead me away!

COUNT HOHENZOLLERN

   My Elector, can your heart — ?

THE PRINCE OF HOMBURG (*tearing himself away*)

                  You tyrants, would you

   drag me in chains out to the firing squad?

   Away! I've made my reckoning with the world.

   (*Exit with the* GUARD.)

NATALIA (*laying her head against the* ELECTRESS' *bosom*)

   O earth, receive me now into your midst!

   Why should I see the sunlight any longer?

SCENE NINE

The same, without the PRINCE OF HOMBURG.

MARSHAL DÖRFLING

   God of the world! Must it then come to this?

   (*The* ELECTOR *speaks urgently and in secret with an*
   OFFICER.)

COLONEL KOTTWITZ (*coldly*)

   My Lord and Sovereign, after what has happened,

   are we dismissed?

THE ELECTOR

             No, not yet at this time.

   You will be told when you're dismissed.

(*He stares at him for a moment. Then he picks up the papers the* PAGE *has brought him and turns to* MARSHAL DÖRFLING.)

Here, Marshal:
the passport for the Swedish Count of Horn!
Tell him it is the Prince's wish, my cousin's,
which I'm in duty bound to carry out;
the war will start again in three days' time.
(*Pause. He glances at the death sentence.*)
Judge yourselves, gentlemen: The Prince of Homburg
this past year, by his wanton recklessness,
has taken two impressive victories from me
and seriously infringed upon a third;
now, with the experience of these days behind him,
will you a fourth time take your chance with him?

COLONEL KOTTWITZ *and* COUNT TRUCHSS (*simultaneously*)
What did you say, my wonderful, adored —

THE ELECTOR
Will you? Will you?

KOTTWITZ
Sire, by the living God,
you might be standing at the brink of ruin
and he would not now even draw his sword
to aid or save you unsolicited!

THE ELECTOR (*tearing up the death sentence*)
Follow me then, my friends, into the garden!
(*exeunt*)

SCENE TEN

*Castle with a ramp leading down into the garden, as in Act
One. It is night again*
THE PRINCE OF HOMBURG, *blindfolded, is led through
the lower gate by* CAPTAIN STRANZ. OFFICERS *with a* GUARD.
Drums of a funeral march are heard in the distance.

THE PRINCE OF HOMBURG

Now, immortality, you're wholly mine!
You're shining through the fillet of my eyes,
resplendent, toward the multifarious sun.
I'm growing wings on both my shoulders now;
my spirit swings through still, ethereal spaces;
and, as a ship sped by the breath of wind
observes the cheerful port become submerged,
so, dimly, all that lives goes under for me.
Now I distinguish color yet and form,
and now all lies beneath me in a mist.
(*He sits down on the bench in the center, at the oak tree.*
CAPTAIN STRANZ *moves away, looking up to the ramp.*)

THE PRINCE OF HOMBURG

Oh, what a lovely smell of mignonettes!
You notice it?

STRANZ (*returning*)

                    They're pinks and gillyflowers.

THE PRINCE OF HOMBURG

Pinks? How did they get here?

STRANZ

                    I do not know.
It looks as if some girl has planted them.
Here: would you like to have a gillyflower?

THE PRINCE OF HOMBURG

Thank you! At home I'll put it in some water.

SCENE ELEVEN

The ELECTOR, *holding the wreath of laurel leaves entwined with the golden chain, the* ELECTRESS, PRINCESS NATALIA, MARSHAL DÖRFLING, COLONEL KOTTWITZ, COUNT HOHEN-ZOLLERN, CAPTAIN GOLZ, *and so forth,* LADIES-IN-WAITING, OFFICERS, *and* PAGES *with torches appear on the ramp of the castle.* HOHENZOLLERN *steps to the ramp with a handkerchief and waves to* CAPTAIN STRANZ. *The latter leaves the* PRINCE OF HOMBURG *and speaks with the* GUARD *in the background.*

THE PRINCE OF HOMBURG

What is this spreading brillance? Can you tell me?

CAPTAIN STRANZ (*returning*)

My Prince, would you be kind enough to rise?

THE PRINCE OF HOMBURG

What is it?

STRANZ

Nothing that should frighten you:

I merely want to bare your eyes again.

THE PRINCE OF HOMBURG

Is this the final hour of my misfortunes?

STRANZ

It is indeed. God bless you: you deserve it!

(*The* ELECTOR *gives the wreath and chain to* NATALIA, *takes her by the hand, and leads her down the ramp. The*

GENTLEMEN *and* LADIES *follow. Surrounded by torches,* NATALIA *steps before the* PRINCE, *who rises amazed. She puts the wreath on his head and the chain around his neck and presses his hand to her heart. The* PRINCE *faints.)*

PRINCESS NATALIA

Heavens, the joy is killing him.

COUNT HOHENZOLLERN (*raising the* PRINCE)

To rescue!

THE ELECTOR

Let the artillery thunder wake him up!

(*Gun salvos. A march. Lights go up in the castle.*)

COLONEL KOTTWITZ

Hail, hail the Prince of Homburg!

THE OFFICERS

Hail, hail, hail!

ALL

Victorious in the battle at Fehrbellin!

(*brief pause*)

THE PRINCE OF HOMBURG

No, say: Is this a dream?

KOTTWITZ

A dream! What else?

SEVERAL OFFICERS

Into the field!

COUNT TRUCHSS

To battle!

MARSHAL DÖRFLING

On to victory!

ALL

Down with all enemies of Brandenburg!

CURTAIN